PICK ME!

Loving and Living with People You Just Don't Get

Lynne Schinella

For Mum and Dad, who showed me what love is.

Contents

Introduction

In the beginning, it's perfect.
You love their ability to socialise.
You love that cute little tummy.
You love that they motivate you to be a better person …

Love. It's a grand thing. I'm a big fan. But then, as a Mango with a Banana rising, I've got love to give out in bucket loads and I'm particularly good at it—smothering—some have said. But falling in love can be addictive. That feeling of euphoria, butterflies, excitement, and happiness is all down to some pretty cool science happening in the background.

Dr Helen Fisher is a US-based biological anthropologist. She has conducted extensive research and written six books on the evolution and future of sex, love, marriage, and gender differences in the brain, how your personality style shapes who you are, and who you love. Fisher says when we start falling in love, our brains release chemicals such as adrenaline, oxytocin, and dopamine that set our neural receptors on fire and give us a sense of euphoria and purpose.[1] It's almost like you've had a few drinks where the oxytocin lowers your

---

[1] A Moor, 2018, *This is what Happens to Your Body When you Fall in Love*, Best Life, viewed 2nd September 2020, <https://bestlifeonline.com/what-happens-to-your-body-when-you-fall-in-love/>

inhibitions and makes you more confident and outgoing. Nothing can go wrong! We fall in love with our partner's smell—those damned persuasive pheromones, and float around wearing their shirt.

If you're unapologetically romantic like me, you'll enjoy the findings of this Californian study. Emilio Ferrer, a psychology professor from the University of California, Davis, conducted a series of studies on couples in romantic relationships and reported they could share experiences at a physiological level. The study found that couples in love could synchronise their heartbeats and breathing patterns when sitting close enough to each other. We breathe as one.[2] Aww …

Time passes …

Why do we always have to be with other people? I just want a night in.

What's with that tummy? Fat bastard.

Why are you always on my back to do stuff? I'm not like you. Let me take my time.

So how do we make this work given the natural passing of time? In my lifetime, I've been lucky enough to fall deeply in love twice, and in a more, let's say, playful way dozens of times (more than Mother Theresa, less than Russell Brand). I am a great believer that when you've got something good going on, it's worth working for. And it *is* work.

---

[2] E Ferrer, 2013, *Lovers' hearts beat in sync, UC Davis study says*, University of California, viewed 2 September 2020 <https://www.ucdavis.edu/news/lovers-hearts-beat-sync-uc-davis-study-says/>

Nearly twenty years ago, I was introduced to different personality types. It changed my life, professionally and personally. By understanding more about myself, my strengths, and flaws, and by understanding more about other people, I now had a compass to guide me. The better the ability to get inside our partner's head and see things from their perspective, the greater the chance of a successful relationship. There's more respect, less stress, and extra time for the good things in life.

Personality and behavioural profiling is not new. It dates back to Ancient Greece, more than 2,500 years ago, when philosopher and medic Hippocrates[3] (460–370 BC) proposed a medical theory that there were only four different humours, as he called them, based on a balance of bodily fluids: black bile, yellow bile, phlegm, and blood. According to this balance of fluids, we'd behave in a certain way. Later, Roman philosopher and medic Galen (AD 129–c. 200) named these temperaments as Choleric, Sanguine, Melancholic, and Phlegmatic.[3]

The idea gained in popularity through the ages and formed the basis of all the personality and behavioural profiling in the last 150 years, entering the popular psyche mid 20th century, when well known Myers Briggs Type Indicator was developed originally to help women in World War II identify jobs that would best suit them.[4]

[3] A Jesper Dammeyer, Ingo Zettler, 2018, *A Brief Historical Overview on Links Between Personality and Health*, Personality and Disease, viewed 2nd October 2020 <https://www.sciencedirect.com/topics/psychology/four-temperament>

[4] Isobel Briggs Meyers, 2020, The Meyers Briggs Foundation, viewed 2nd October 2020, <https://www.myersbriggs.org/my-mbti-personality-type/mbti-basics/isabel-briggs-myers.htm>

In 2004, I created a behavioural profiling tool around four personality types called Apples, Mangoes, Limes, and Bananas, in response to a growing need for information delivered simply. The fruit theme made sense as my company is called RIPE and it was originally intended for the workplace to better aid respectful, clear workplace communication. In 2012, my book *Bite Me! And Other Do's and Don'ts of Dealing with our Differences* was published as a useful guide for working with people you just don't get and introducing the Fruit personalities. The first four chapters in Part One of this book are an update on those in Bite Me. It was soon evident, however, that this information resonates well beyond the office. Every time I deliver a conference keynote or workshop, people come up to me to discuss their partners. So it was that this book evolved, fuelled by real stories, from real people.

Some of us choose our partners by compiling a list of desirable traits and searching for our perfect match on dating apps, some of us simply fall for someone because we feel it in our bones. Regardless of how we find a partner, we are all prone to one mistake: believing we can change the bits we don't particularly like.

Cute Tummy has become Fat Bastard. You put together a plan and sign them up for a gym membership, but we all know they will buy the latest lycra®, go once or twice, and then get bored. You have told them over and over why they should aim higher, be more disciplined, achieve more. You have *told* them. So why can't they just do it?

Unless someone chooses to change, there will *be* no change on your watch. None. Once you understand this, you have one choice, my friends, *to love your partner for who they are.* And this means knowing their strengths and the traits you think of as flaws and working out how it'll work with your own attributes and quirks.

For this, you'll need your secret superpower: empathy.

Empathy makes us human. It gives us the ability to connect and relate to others and allows us to back off when we recognise our own behaviour becoming gnarly or inappropriate. Some Fruit types, such as Bananas, have empathy by the kilo. Apples, on the other hand, are somewhat deficient in the empathy gene. If we're going to foster and maintain serious romantic partnerships, **then empathy is our secret superpower.**

Demonstrating empathy in our relationships can be tough as we tend to save our worst behaviour for the people we love the most because we know they'll forgive us. How easy is it to get upset with your significant other when you're tired or under pressure? You snap. You don't feel like apologising because, seriously, this is something they do all the time. *I'm too tired to explain myself again. Maybe next time you might actually get it.* All arguments, even if they're over replacing the toilet roll, are because something else has been building up. It's never just the toilet roll.

Learning about Fruit personalities gives you a blameless language to communicate with. It won't solve all your problems, but knowledge of your different traits allows you to put the brakes on before it gets ugly. You can't use your Fruit preference as an excuse. I'm a Mango—I can't do that! I'm a Lime, sorry, but I'm the wrong person for that job. We are all capable of wearing any Fruit hat we choose. Okay, the hat may not sit as well as some, but we can still do it.

I'm from Sydney, Australia, and when my marriage broke up, my husband and I were living in the city of Brisbane, 1,000 kilometres away from Sydney. We had two boys and chose to have the boys stay with each parent on alternate weeks. Rather than sit in misery the week my children were not with me, I realised I'd be happier in Sydney where my family, friends, and business network were. Then I met a man. In Sydney. And so began thirteen years of living in alternate cities. Every second Monday morning, I would take the boys to school, fly to Sydney, clean the house, do the grocery shopping, and live my Sydney life. A week later I'd fly back, clean the Brisbane house, do the grocery shopping, and pick up the kids. To say I was a little confused is an understatement. Tuck shop mother in Brisbane, sex goddess in Sydney. And you never want to get the two mixed up. The point is, it is possible to switch hats depending on circumstances, your partner, and your stage in life—all of which we'll talk about later in the book. Unlike a business relationship, in a personal relationship we have the opportunity to clash on almost every level of being together, and our different Fruit personalities make this very clear.

Social

Apples won't tolerate idiots in their lives.
Mangoes want to go out anywhere, any day.
Limes just need alone time.
Bananas always let you choose; they never decide.

Household Chores

Apples delegate.
Mangoes buy milk when it runs out.

Limes rule over household duties.

Bananas clean when they can no longer stand the mess.

Finance

Apples are all over it as long as they have control.

Mangoes spend until their credit card is knocked back.

Limes are detailed spreadsheet experts.

Bananas hope someone else will do it.

Sex

Apples like efficiency and time constraints.

Mangoes like it on the dining table.

Limes like schedules to prepare.

You will never find Bananas through the scattered rose petals and soft lighting.

And when things go pear-shaped

Apples can resort to physical intimidation, fear, and control.

Mangoes can use emotional seduction, mental manipulation, and sarcasm.

Limes opt for the silent treatment, blame, and superiority.

Bananas go for tears, guilt, and submissiveness.

So much to learn!

Understanding each other's strengths, challenges, needs, and wants helps cut arguments and tension off at the pass to avoid sliding into nastiness. Learning the Fruit language allows us to defuse a potential blow up and, instead, have a respectful conversation—even if it is difficult. After all, when you ask someone to take off their Apple hat and bring out their inner Banana, you must at least smile a bit because Fruit personalities are silly.

Each one of us is a magnificent, complex blend of more than 20,000 different genes[5]—and this is scratching the surface. The personality we were born with simply forms the foundation of who we are, and how we behave. On top of that, we layer our experiences, ethnicity, generation, culture, religion, gender, and ability.

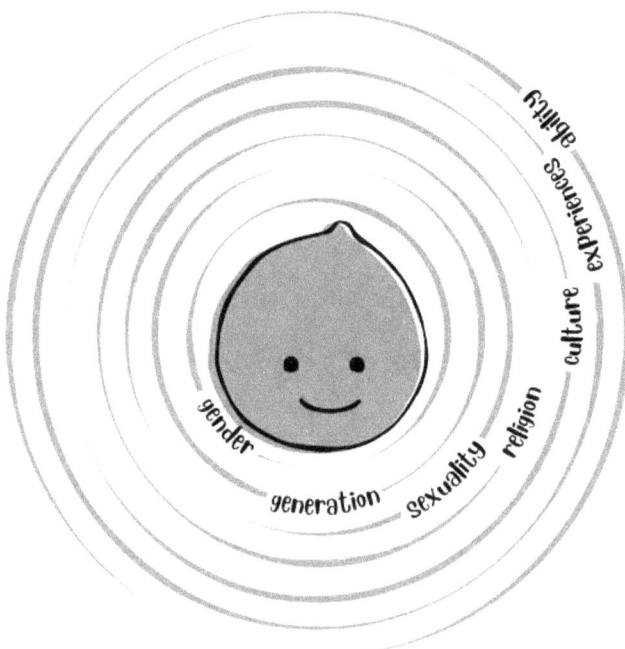

Image 1: The layers of diversity above the foundation of personality who make us who we are

---

5 US National Library of Medicine, *What is a gene?*, viewed 2 September 2020, <https://ghr.nlm.nih.gov/primer/basics/gene>

Clearly understanding how our personalities affect our behaviour is not going to magically make our relationships brilliant, but it's a damn good start.

How To Read This Book

To get all the good stuff in both enjoyment and learning in this book, stop now and do the quiz – Which Fruit are you? to find out what Fruit blend both you and your partner are. Then get ready to laugh and learn how you can love and live better together.

Go here to do the quiz: https://lynneschinella.com.au/book-quiz

Then get ready to laugh and learn how you can love and live better together.

1. Do the quiz
2. Part One – read it all
3. Part Two – head to the sections and stories relating to you and your partner's first preference. Anything else is a bonus.

Once you've done the quiz and figured out what your Fruity preferences are, make sure you read the first four chapters which explain the Fruit basics. Don't just read your own, Apples. Your results profile what percentage of each Fruit you are, and your natural preferences, and you may also recognise some of your traits in the other Fruit types, which I'll explain in the chapter on Fruit Blends. Then again, if you are an Apple, you might want to shoot straight to the summaries at the end of each chapter.

When it comes to Part Two - Fruit Pairings (how the personality types interact with each other in a relationship) **each of the four stories plays out with four different scenarios, depending on the pairing.**

For example, if your first preference is Apple and your partner is a Lime, head to the Apple section and read the Apple and Lime story. Then take your second preference and read that story—if your second preference is Lime, read Lime with Lime.

I've used examples of extreme Fruit personalities in each of the stories, for two reasons. One, it's funnier. Two, extreme cases better illustrate the point, make the traits easier to recall. Every anecdote is a true story. I've just cobbled the anecdotes together to create extremes.

Please remember if you are suffering any mental health issues, or serious problems in your relationship, it is important to seek professional help. Please don't hesitate.

This book simply provides a blameless language to use when things go pear-shaped, but it is not a substitute for professional counselling. We are complicated creatures, and relationships are hard work; even for those of us with high emotional intelligence. When you find someone you love, don't let it go easily.

A short word on parenting.

This is not a book on parenting, but I know many of you will see Fruity traits in your children, and I hope this helps navigate the wild ride. We are born with a natural set of traits which become more layered through nurturing and experience. In certain circumstances, life experience can alter our natural traits.

This is clear with young children in a day care centre. Some children stomp around the sandpit ensuring they get the best toys. Some laugh and swing dangerously from the highest branch. Others arrange pencils in neat rows. And some are holding hands and hugging. I've seen the differences in my own children, how they were as little ones, and who they've become as men, moulded through different experiences but retaining the very essence of who they are.

For parents reading this book, here are some words of encouragement. Parenting is a big old challenge no matter what Fruit you and your children are. No two people will parent in the same way. You will argue a lot over parenting techniques, whether you're both biological parents, parenting a stepchild (straight to heaven for you lot), or two separated biological parents. Whether you are straight or gay, black, white, brown, or yellow; it doesn't matter. It's just damned hard.

Trust yourself that you are providing a strong foundation. Trust that you are doing the absolute best you can. You are doing great.

What does it all mean for you and your partner? In the first section, we'll take a look at each Fruit in its extremes as if there is one imaginary pure Fruit. Extremes are the easiest way to remember and recognise traits.

But remember that no one is just one Fruit. As your profile results will show, we are a delicious blend of all four Fruit, with a preference for one, two, and sometimes even three types. Although we can use traits from each of the four fruit, we tend to work in our top two preferences. More on this in Chapter Five on Fruity Blends.

Another important reminder: **this is unashamedly Pop Psychology (popular psychology)**.

There are sophisticated profiling systems around which deliver a detailed personality analysis. This book is designed to be easily digested, and to provide simple, memorable guidelines to recognise traits in yourself and your partner to help you love and live better together.

Let's do this.

Which Fruit Are You?

Tick just one option ACROSS each row that best describes you. Add up all the ticks in the column to see what your Fruit preference is.

FAST THINKER	THINKS RANDOMLY	DEEP THINKER	STEADY THINKER
FACTUAL	STORYTELLER	GOOD LISTENER	EMPATHIC
LIKES CONTROL	LIKES VARIETY	LIKES STRUCTURE	LIKES DIRECTION
OPINIONATED	INSPIRATIONAL	STABILISING	TEAM PLAYER
QUICK DECISIONS	SPONTANEOUS	PROCRASTINATES	HESITANT
COMPETITIVE	ENTHUSIASTIC	ACCURATE	EASY GOING
INDEPENDENT	GENEROUS	CAREFUL	LOYAL
LIKES RESULTS	LIKES FUN	LIKES RULES	LIKES HARMONY
LOGICAL	CHARISMATIC	ORGANISED	KIND
BUSINESS LIKE	SELF DEPRACATING	PERFECTIONIST	RELAXED
DIRECT	OPEN	MODEST	GENUINE
LIKES TO WORK	LIKES TO PARTY	LIKES TO BE NEAT	LIKES TO CHILL
INTOLERANT	IDEALISTIC	PESSIMISTIC	CAN'T SAY NO
BIG PICTURE	BORED EASILY	DETAILED	GOOD LISTENER
ORGANISED	UNDISCIPLINED	EFFICIENT	CASUAL
CONFIDENT	FORGIVING	LOYAL	FLEXIBLE
DOMINANT	PASSIONATE	ANALYTICAL	HUMBLE
ADVENTUROUS	FLEXIBLE	CREATIVE	DIPLOMATIC
OUTSPOKEN	SHOW OFF	RESERVED	ACCOMMODATING
RESOURCEFUL	FEARLESS	CAUTIOUS	CONSISTENT
ARGUMENTATIVE	SELF FOCUSED	OVERLY SENSITIVE	PASSIVE AGGRESSIVE
ACTION ORIENTED	FREE SPIRIT	CALCULATED	PEACEMAKER
SOLVES	MOTIVATES	WORRIES	GIVES
DISLIKES SLOWNESS	DISLIKES NEGATIVITY	DISLIKES TALKERS	DISLIKES AGGRESSION
FEARS LOSING CONTROL	FEARS NOT BEING LIKED	FEARS EMBARRASSMENT	FEARS CONFLICT
POLITICAL	OPEN MINDED	COMPETENT	FRIENDLY
IMPATIENT	DISRESPECTFUL OF RULES	OVERLY CRITICAL	AVOIDS SPEAKING UP
ACCEPTS CHANGE	THRIVES ON CHANGE	SUSPICIOUS OF CHANGE	NERVOUS OF CHANGE
APPLE	**MANGO**	**LIME**	**BANANA**

PART ONE
FRUIT BASICS

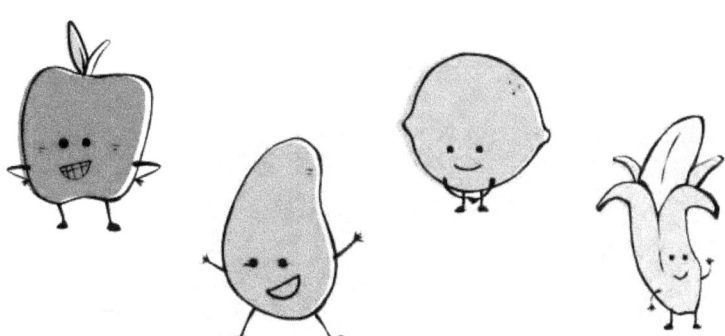

Awesome Apples

Apple at a Glance

Likes	Dislikes
results	incompetence
achievement	lack of thought
challenge	those who don't speak up
competition	those who don't keep up
work	inaction
Good bits	**Not-so-good bits**
quick decision-making	unemotional
intelligent	argumentative
action-oriented	prone to aggression
Communication	**Motivation**
relevant facts	control
brevity	independence
fast talker	power
can attack	
believe they're always right	

With their strong left-brained skills of logic and analysis, the Apple is often found leading companies and countries. Apples get things done while they're doing twelve other things at the same time. The Apple is business-like, functional, and well-organised. They think quickly and efficiently and become frustrated with those who can't keep up. They can be impatient and can't understand why others don't "get it" the first time.

The Apple has an intrinsic need to be in control, regardless of whether it's their business unit or their family. Their way is the best way. Losing control is what they fear most.

Apples must win at all costs. They must win the conversation and have the last word. Apples are incredibly tenacious. Giving up doesn't enter into their consciousness. If all else fails, they often bully their way forward until everyone else just gives in for the sake of peace. It's fairly obvious that when they arrive home, they need a much gentler approach.

An admirable Apple trait is believing they can overcome any obstacle and dominate in any field. Sure, they may encounter a few landmines along the way, but with some careful defusing, they will reach their goal. This self-belief can make them seem arrogant, but it's not meant that way; it's just fact.

A special friend of mine always wanted to write a book. That the publishing industry is cut-throat and thousands of would-be authors write manuscripts which never get looked at, let alone published, didn't faze her. She knew she could write a great story and she did. Her first manuscript was accepted, and she's now written more than forty novels across several genres. I marvel at that absolute self-belief. This doesn't mean she's arrogant or vain. She doesn't boast of her achievements. She just knows she's good.

Apples also pride themselves on being able to deal with the many tasks they set themselves. Nothing is beyond them.

They don't just want to be okay at it, though; they want to master every skill. They particularly enjoy being better than everyone else. The intense desire to achieve is a constant companion to the Apple, who puts pressure on themselves and those around them. Their constant obsession with achievement can cause tension at home as they struggle with the high bar they set themselves.

They risk coming unstuck when they don't achieve the results they want. Apples have enormously high expectations of themselves—and others, for that matter. Failure is not an option, but if it does happen, you'll never hear a word about it. Whatever they attempt, there can be no backsliding. They have to keep getting better and are merciless in their self-condemnation.

Apples are equally brutal when it comes to others underachieving in their eyes. Apple parents take no prisoners. Children of Apples will end up being high achievers all their lives, or rebel completely.

Because an Apple is so results driven it is easy for them to put other elements that are important in a relationship, like pleasing others and caring about feelings, as a lower priority. The Apple feels strongly about the inner circle of people closest to them, including their children and anyone else able to sneak under the radar. They'll fight to the death for those people, but if you don't fit in this category, don't expect a whole lot of loving. Apples love to solve and fix. By the same token, they want to hear how much you love them to solve and fix.

These high left-brain thinkers have a wonderful gift of critical analysis. They can analyse a situation rapidly, toss around all the possible solutions, and clearly see the most effective one—all in the time it would take us lesser mortals to understand the initial problem. Being able to see a problem with such clarity also allows Apples to get maximum results for minimum effort, which is just the way they like it. **They *hate* wasted effort.**

At their worst, a bad Apple can become highly critical, taking the feelings of others and grinding them into the ground. Being pragmatists to the core, they simply see it as solving the problem and are not always aware of the hurt they may be causing. The next time you see two Apples engaged in heated debate, don't stop to feel bad for them, they're loving it! For them, they're on the dance floor. They're at the bar knocking back a few beers. They're shooting some baskets. They see it as an opportunity to mentally engage another active, intelligent mind and they find argument energising, even if the rest of us don't.

Apples are efficient machines. They don't use up fuel unnecessarily. That means they don't overeat. If they want to lose weight, they're efficient, goal-oriented, and want to do it fast because time is precious. They want you to keep up with their frenetic pace, and when you can't, they get frustrated. Some of the other Fruit may need a break, but the Apple is ready to go full pelt all night just to get the job done.

Recognise a boss you may have had? They don't waste words, preferring to avoid the irrelevant, the trivial, and the redundant – just get straight to the point. They're reluctant to state the obvious and assume that if it's obvious to them, then it should be to you. To an Apple, chatting about the weather, small talk, and thinking out loud is a waste of breath.

You only make a mistake once around an Apple. Although they are kinder at home than they are at work, they are scathing and unforgiving when it comes to error in themselves and others. Stupidity is a crime. Even at home, the Apple prefers to keep emotions in check, which allows them to maintain control. They don't trust easily, and you'll need both trust and logic when it comes to arguments. The big challenge for Apples is to grow their relatively small empathy gene and to cut the rest of the Fruit a bit of slack.

The thing I love about Apples though, is their directness and their intelligence. With an Apple, you always know where you stand: no pussyfooting around, no pretence, and no back-stabbing. You might not like what you hear up front, but at least you can deal with reality.

Spot the Apple

You can recognise an Apple by their blunt, direct speech. They speak quickly and to the point. If you have an Apple in your life, you'll often feel like they're grilling you or not showing enough interest. Their speech is compact, crisp, and sometimes terse, and then they wonder why they've lost their audience. To others, it may seem rude; to an Apple, succinct words and phrases get to the point more efficiently. Apples often interrupt if you're not speaking quickly enough or if they're bored with what you're saying, and have no problem with appearing confrontational, even on first meeting.

Apples appear confident. They stand tall and straight and will look you directly in the eye. Chins are uplifted. Likewise, they use strong body language; you may see closed or pounding fists or pointing fingers. They dress efficiently—even to a barbeque. They will look business-like because they're always ready for action. And if you're really stuck, find about how they spend their time. If they're General Manager of an ASX100 company with two small children, accompanying their partner to corporate dinners, and completing an MBA or PhD, chances are you've struck a Golden Delicious.

So how do I deal with Apples?

Some may argue that Apples are the most difficult Fruit to get on with, but that's only when you don't understand them.

There are three key drivers when you want to get through to an Apple:

- they fear losing control
- they need intellectual stimulation
- they must work towards goal-oriented results.

Let these factors be your Apple GPS. When you want something from an Apple, these simple rules will improve your chances:

Have your facts. If you don't, they'll eat you for breakfast. Have a logical argument that flows. Play them with reason.

Speak quickly. Give them the facts logically, but don't labour the point: make it fast. If you're not quick enough, they'll move on to the next subject.

Go head to head. For most Fruit, Apples are toughest when they bring out their inner bully, intentional or not. This can include raising their voice, strong body language, invading your space, and making demands you can't meet. When it comes to a difference of opinion or an argument, you'd better be on your toes. You are much better off going head to head with an Apple, as scary as that might sound. You see, an Apple quite likes a bit of verbal fencing. They see it as sport, and they're good at it. I have asked hundreds of Apples in my audiences whether, when they start to argue, they want people to run off scared, or stay and take them on. The verdict is unanimous. Fight.

Apples want you to stand up to them. This can be a scary proposition. Apples can articulate themselves well; but all Apples agree that if you stand up to them, you have more chance of developing a mutually respectful, long-term relationship.

Apples see it as a weakness when you don't hold your ground, and while they may not show it, they grudgingly admit respect for anyone that does. This doesn't mean matching them with raised voices and a belligerent attitude, if that's what is happening. It means being firm and calm and letting them know where you stand on a subject, what you're prepared to tolerate, and what is unacceptable.

Sound hard? It can be. But start practicing on some small new season Delicious and lead up to the Big Hard Grannies. It'll get easier.

How Apples See Themselves

How Apples see themselves	How others can see Apples
determined	bloody-minded
results-driven	slave driver
hardworking	workaholic
smart	smart
confident	arrogant
direct	rude
pragmatic	uncaring
efficient	controlling

Short and Sweet

Apple Characteristics

- logical
- big-picture analysis
- quick thinkers
- need control
- like making their own rules
- love to win
- high achievers
- results at any cost
- obsessed with family
- enjoy conflict
- appear unemotional
- unwavering self-belief
- intellectual
- pragmatic.

Spot the Apple

- direct
- business-like
- ask a lot of questions
- confident
- direct speech
- punch out words
- eyes that grill you
- strong body language.

Dealing with Apples

- have your facts ready
- speak quickly
- get to the point
- back up argument with logic
- do not run away.

Chapter 2

Magnificent Mangoes

Mango at a Glance

Likes	Dislikes
fun	rules
variety	negativity
new ideas	small-mindedness
change	detail

Good bits	Not-so-good bits
positive	disorganised
generous	lack of respect for rules
forgiving	self-absorbed

Communication	Motivation
visuals	being liked and recognised
metaphors	status
storytelling	desire to make a difference
speaks quickly	
random jumping between topics	
sarcastic under attack	

Mangoes have more flavour and colour than any of the other Fruit. Everything is bigger and brighter, from their music to their food. Mangoes are fabulous—just ask them! They're the ones at the party, surrounded by people laughing at their funny stories and warm manner while they exaggerate and gesture wildly to get more of a laugh. They look good and are dressed in the latest fashion.

Right-brained Mangoes are natural storytellers. Too many of them at a dinner party and you'll never get a word in. Mangoes are loved and adored for their charisma and extroversion or reviled and abhorred for their flamboyance and inability to take life seriously. It just depends which Fruit is looking at them. Life's just too much fun for a Mango. They see excitement in everything, living for today because you could be dead tomorrow.

A strong Mango draws people to them, because they always seem to be the ones having a good time. They are self-confident and charming which helps to make them great motivators. Mangoes enjoy people around them but not if it brings conflict. Not that they shy away from conflict, they just see argument as a bit of a waste. Why argue when you could be having fun? They handle arguments as quickly as possible, so they can move on to the fun bit. They have generous natures and like to help solve problems, whether it's giving their time or their money. The motive for this and solving arguments is simple: let's be quick, so we can move on to the next exciting thing.

Mangoes can make you feel like you're the only person in the room, as if you're their best friend. And you are, until you're not. This is not intentional—it's just that Mangoes live in the present; they live for the now. This is positive, in that by living in the present, Mangoes can forgive quickly and move on. Not so positive—they are not deep, introspective thinkers who spend a long time reflecting on their mistakes. Whether they reverse the new car into a pole or lose the deal at the negotiating table, there's no time for moping; they pick themselves up and move on. And because they don't always take the time to analyse those mistakes, it means that sometimes they don't learn from them.

Battling weight gain is common for this Fruit. I mean, how can they possibly resist all of life's sensual food pleasures? It's a real struggle for the Mango, who has a substantial ego and wants to look good, against the desire to have the jewels of caviar burst on the tongue or the silky indulgence of a zabaglione slip down the throat. After all, life is for living!

The Mango has a general propensity to be accident-prone. Mangoes are the Fruit that are thinking continuously, moving quickly, and along the way can stub a toe, bruise a hip, or knock over a glass. They take a cavalier approach to all of this. After all, if they don't do it quickly, they might miss out on the next exciting thing just around the corner!

Mangoes are intrinsically optimistic creatures. Even when something goes wrong in a Mango world, they are quick to see what good can come out of it. A Mango who loses a leg will be grateful that they can save money on shoes. An admirable trait, although not always realistic.

Mangoes, like Apples, believe anything can be achieved. They don't have the same unwavering self-belief; however, they trust that there is always a way around a problem. Obstacles other people would consider impossible to overcome, the Mango sees as a challenge. Because of their openness to change and new ideas, they'll consider anything it takes to get a successful outcome. Anything except, perhaps, the fine print. Mangoes are consistently bad at reading instructions, completing forms, and filling out warranty cards.

You've got it—they're not great on detail ... Mangoes are big-picture people.

Mangoes are visionaries. They possess the wonderful gift of being able to imagine something in 3D and see no need to fret about details. They think in pictures, which is why their faces may suddenly go blank if you're talking statistics. This ability to translate everything into pictures also means they can choose to laugh at the oddest times. They're seeing something in their heads that you're not.

You don't often meet a wealthy Mango. They may look the part with their designer clothes and up-to-the-minute accessories, overflowing with confidence. But—don't tell anyone—most of it's on credit. Because the Mango loves to spend and to have a great time, savings are put off until another day and debts pile up. Mangoes need to work on the discipline gene or at least have someone around them to pick up the slack. And I do mean *slack*.

They don't like to be reminded of how much something costs while they're having a good time, because they've already taken the risk, are enjoying themselves, and don't want to think about the harsh realities of paying off a credit card later. They're notorious for planning big surprises, parties, or trips and worrying about the money afterwards. In their mind, afterwards may never come. They are spontaneous and impulsive creatures.

Mangoes are inspirational people who get those around them excited about a new project. The trouble is, the same Mangoes get bored quickly. Strong Mangoes are extremely clever at starting many projects and then getting others to finish them.

I have a great friend who excels in this. I watch in awe as people around her make curtains, wash floors, run committees, do research, and get festivals up and running. Men and women alike fall under her special Mango charm.

Because of their openness to new ideas, Mangoes are the best at adapting to change. They love new challenges and are great at saying, "Yes!" to taking on a last-minute project. Just make sure you have some detail-oriented people around for back up. This ability to adapt also allows Mangoes to work well when it comes to a crisis. They are the most likely of all the Fruit to go with the flow and land on their feet. And if they land on their knees instead of their feet, their optimistic nature allows them to see the good to come out of it as if they'd planned it all along.

Someone with strong Mango traits has a gnawing desire to have social impact, to be able to help the world and change it in some way for the better. Their natural generosity spills over to make their home, workplace, community, or world a better place.

This fat fruit has huge emotional needs—a desire to love and be loved. They can't get enough affection and need frequent interaction with family and friends. It upsets them when people don't like them—they just can't understand why: I mean, what's not to like?

A trait that has the other Fruit puzzled, if not embarrassed, is the Mangoes desire to talk about anything that happened in their day, no matter how awkward. This is because they see it as funny; they relish the opportunity to retell a story and get a laugh. Others are mortified. The Mango's ability to be self-deprecating can be endearing. They readily admit mistakes and allow themselves to be seen as human. Because they have an underlying unshakeable confidence, they don't think that other people will hold these mistakes against them. Here they are underestimating our Lime friends, who remember everything and play the video over and over again.

But if a Mango is telling a story about something bad that's happened to them and it's not funny, remember: they don't need it solved (Apples) and they don't need you to rant and rave. They just need a hug.

These are the things I love best about Mangoes: their positive attitude, their willingness to change, and their ability to forgive and move on.

Spot the Mango

Mangoes often stand out because they're talking quickly and enthusiastically and using their hands a lot. In fact, all their body language is open. They look well-off and well-dressed but watch for tell-tale signs of rushing around doing too many things at once. This usually takes the form of sloppiness in dress—a pulled thread, a missing button, a coffee stain. If you quiz them about it, they'll exclaim, 'It was fine when I left home this morning!' even it if wasn't.

A Mango's speech is free-flowing and playful, and they have a full vocal range which they use animatedly. They don't often take a breath and you may notice many of the stories they tell are about them. Their thoughts can seem random, like a pinball machine, ricocheting from one subject to another. If you're talking, they may get fidgety. Watch for the signs when their eyes glaze over or they start shifting. They'll be busting at the seams to say something, because what they've got to say is always far more interesting!

Mangoes have an easy smile and a tendency to make people feel comfortable around them. Their eyes are wide open and dancing, really interested in what you have to say ... until they're not.

So how do I deal with Mangoes?

As with anyone, it helps your chances of connecting if you know their key drivers. Mangoes care most about:

- variety: looking for new and interesting things to do
- fun
- recognition
- being liked.

So when you need something from a Mango, bear these values in mind.

Be direct. The casual attitude of a Mango can be terribly frustrating to the more structured Fruit (hello Limes). Mangoes can easily get up a Lime's nose by talking too much, talking over the top of them, finishing their sentences, and just being fabulous. The good news is that of all the Fruit, Mangoes are the most self-deprecating, and when you draw attention to their shortcomings, they will most likely agree with you. You can bet that someone has told them the same thing before. Tell a Mango to take a breath and give someone else some space, in direct terms, and they'll take it in their stride.

Praise them. They love recognition and are not averse to having their egos stroked.

Talk big picture: Don't bog them down with detail. Mangoes are opportunists—this goes with their key driver of variety; looking for new and interesting things to do. If you're trying to sell them on a thought, whether to go out for a Thai dinner or smarten up on the cleaning, convince them of the pay-off and you're in.

Be fast. To keep their interest, talk quickly. They expect you to be stimulating, just as they think they are.

Pull them back on track when they lose focus. When they invariably wander off the subject, pull them back firmly and don't allow them to digress too much. Once again, Mangoes know this is a bad habit and will be happy to come back to the matter at hand.

Use humour. You can usually use a joke to defuse a potentially difficult situation. With their propensity to put everything into pictures, and their generally positive attitude, Mangoes can usually be counted on to see the funny side.

How Mangoes See Themselves

How Mangoes see themselves	How others can see Mangoes
charismatic	show-off
adventurous	impulsive
open-minded	radical
well-connected	name-dropper
confident	egotistical
party animal	irresponsible
quick to move on	thoughtless
entertaining	tiresome

Short and Sweet

Mango Characteristics

- storytellers
- charismatic
- live for the moment
- self-confident
- motivational
- generous
- forgiving
- optimistic
- desire to be loved
- adaptable
- big picture
- impulsive
- self-deprecating
- get bored quickly.

Spot the Mango

- talk quickly and a lot
- use their hands to talk, big gestures
- dress in the latest clothes
- free-flowing speech
- dancing eyes, good eye contact
- lots of vocal variety in speech
- make you feel comfortable.

Dealing with a Mango

- be direct
- talk big picture
- praise them
- be fast
- pull them back on track when they lose focus
- use humour.

Chapter 3

Lovely Limes

Lime at a Glance

Likes	Dislikes
planning	people who don't listen
systems	imperfection
a job well done	unpunctuality
rules	rule-breakers
family	unpredictability
Good bits	**Not-so-good bits**
organised	worriers
sensible	judgemental
sensitive	inflexible
Communication	**Motivation**
deliberate words	security
think carefully	accuracy
facts	harmony
specifics	
stubborn in conflict	

Our second left-brained personality, the Limes, are that exotic yet understated Fruit packed with hidden surprises. When you understand a Lime, you will discover their many uses and why they're indispensable in the Fruit bowl. Limes don't show off and they don't stand out. They add flavour to create something special and they don't need to showcase how wonderful they are.

Limes timetables are scheduled to the minute and all their files are in alphabetical order. They don't mince words or waste time on trivia. There is no time for frivolity in a Lime world—everything has to have a purpose. This doesn't mean that they don't have fun; it's just that the fun has to have a purpose. Spontaneity is hard to fathom. The idea that you may act on something that just popped into your head has too many associated risks – including mistakes and embarrassment.

Never expect a Lime to jump for joy when you suggest a weekend away on a Friday morning. What will they wear? Will it be hot or cold? Who will water the plants? They are cautious and deliberate thinkers who need time to consider. Each decision is calculated after thorough analysis.

Limes are worriers by nature. They worry about climate change, whether their hair colour is right for them, and getting dinner on table by 7 pm so the boys can go to football practice. All this worrying can lead to expecting the worst and being quite flat at times. They can be glum and depressed, always assuming poor outcomes. But there's a very positive side to this approach. Because of their nature, Limes are excellent at weeding out any gaps in a plan. The visionary Mango comes up with a big-picture plan that gets everyone excited. The Limes are there to roll their eyes and ask exactly how that three-metre dining table will fit in a two metre space. Without Limes to bring us down to earth, many plans would fail dismally.

Given this careful, slightly anxious approach, they don't like to be around people who are disorganised, late, forgetful, or unpredictable, as this makes Limes feel upset and uneasy. Hello Mangoes.

Limes are careful, composed, conservative, and consistent. You can always depend on a Lime to be there for you. They are loyal and devoted partners.

Limes are perfectionists. Accuracy is all-important for them, so they are happy to spend whatever time it takes to get a job done right. Not preparing and researching is unthinkable. This isn't to impress other people; it's for the Lime's own sanity. A Lime will keep a perfect house. They can't focus on their work unless they know they are coming home to order.

For the rest of us, this can be an absolute bonus, as long as we're patient. Limes get upset with impatience and the desire to simply tick a box to get something done. When Limes are stressed, the people around them become the target of endless nitpicking. They can be quick to judge and, if they don't like someone or something, can close off further communication quickly. The truth is that Limes are sensitive Fruit who get hurt more easily than others. They are crushed by personal criticism, but just don't show it. Because of this propensity to get hurt, they are aware of others' feelings and will never cause pain intentionally.

Limes are awfully responsible and will even take on a responsibility that isn't theirs, out of a sense of duty because no-one else has bothered to volunteer. Unlike the Mango, a Lime will feel a hardened sense of guilt by not offering. They are the keepers of the rules, there to ensure that no-one oversteps the boundaries.

Rule-keeping is fundamental to Lime order. Like their left-brained friends, the Apples, Limes are hard on themselves when they fail, and equally hard on those around them. They are most distressed when rules are broken and order is upset. Turning up late for a meeting or borrowing something and not putting it back in its rightful place can earn stern looks from a Lime.

Because of the rules Limes set themselves though, they are consistent and dependable. A Lime won't let you down when you tell them to be somewhere at 9 am. You want a Lime surgeon for that triple bypass. They rarely complain … out loud. You need to keep a close eye on whether a Lime is happy or not, because they'll usually keep unhappiness to themselves, believing in their glass-half-empty way that complaining is no use.

Limes are super modest and never seek accolades. They hate to draw attention to themselves and find any sort of showing-off almost repugnant. Order and routine represent safety, a key Lime driver.

A Lime I know, and he's not alone, has the same lunch on the same day of the week, every week. He leaves home at the same time and buys his coffee from the same girl at the same café, every day. Routine means less chance of unpredictability or surprises that can upset a Lime's day.

I'll never forget the story a Mango told me of her Lime husband. She was determined to throw him a fortieth birthday party, even though he had insisted he didn't want one. *Impossible!* thought the Mango. Everybody loves a party! She gathered names, ordered cakes and balloons, and organised for everybody to be hiding in the dark when Lime got home from a business trip.

'Surprise!' They shouted as lights went on and cameras flashed.

And Lime's response?

'I told you I didn't want a party,' he said sadly to his Mango wife and walked out.

Don't underestimate the Lime need for privacy and predictability. It needs to be respected.

In confrontation, Limes will often withdraw. They don't like to fight openly, and they feel that if the other party isn't smart enough to see it their way, what's the point of an argument? *Why waste words on someone who'll never get it anyway?* The Lime retreats into moody silence, churning up inside because the other person hasn't realised there's anything wrong.

If you do goad a Lime into an argument, watch while they get ready for a long fight. Like a terrier taking your socks in its mouth, they will not let go. Limes sometimes struggle with new ideas and change brought on quickly, so when they get into a confrontation, they won't budge. Prepare yourself for the long haul.

Money is important to Limes. They keep fuel dockets and council clean-up vouchers, which means they're the smart ones because they end up saving in the long run. They shop during the sales and do as much as they can themselves around the house to save unnecessary spending. They're not tight; they just value money.

Limes are economic in more ways than money. They use words wisely. They like sensible conversation and only speak when they've thought about it and have something of impact to say. Watch for precise, deliberate speech using a limited tonal range.

They see small talk and playful banter as somewhat wasteful, but are also a little envious, as they find this difficult. But on a topic that interests them, they will have a wealth of information which they deliver with great enthusiasm in mindboggling detail. Another Lime will be fascinated, but the people-oriented Mangoes and Bananas will struggle to concentrate with detail overload.

What won't be blindingly obvious to anyone is that many Limes are creative and have a love of aesthetics. Drawing attention to themselves is abhorrent to Limes, so unless you stumble across their talent, you'll never know. Their sensitive, introspective natures are full of deep thoughts and questions. Their energy comes from within, so these emotions can translate into art, music, gardening, cooking, sculpting, or any number of creative pursuits.

What I enjoy about our lovely Limes is their common sense, their skill at planning and order, and their loyal dependability.

Spot the Lime

Limes are easily recognisable because they are meticulous in their appearance: conservative, well-dressed, and neat. I've never seen a Lime with a smear of vegemite from breakfast or a drip of this morning's coffee down their front. You know why? Because they have a spare set of clothes in the car. Extreme Limes couldn't bear the embarrassment of being seen imperfectly in public.

They're likely to be more introverted than extroverted. Limes will make small gestures, keeping their limbs close to their body. When they listen, they're extremely focused, so while it may seem their eyes are scrutinising you, they are just listening carefully.

Their manner is reserved and you won't be able to read a lot of emotions into a Lime face. Their posture can be quite stiff, as they're often wary, ready for fight or flight.

A Lime's immediate environment gives you a good indication of who you're dealing with. Their work desk will have a place for everything, including that hole punch. Work will be set aside neatly and the coffee cup placed in the same spot each day. If you're in a Lime home, you'll know it. Check the wardrobe and marvel at colour-coded shirts, dresses hung by length, and a drawer where the undies are rotated for equal use.

So how do I deal with Limes?

The four things critical to calm in a Lime world are:

- safety
- security
- not making mistakes
- being prepared.

Avoid riding roughshod over a Lime by keeping these key values in mind.

Respect their ways. If you give Limes time to prepare and you understand their immense drive for security, you'll find it much easier to connect. Too many Mangoes scoff at the Lime need for structure and organisation, and the fact they take longer to make a decision.

Don't threaten their safety or security. Of all the Fruit, change is the most challenging for a Lime. When you approach a Lime with a new idea, always be prepared for it to take time to be accepted, whether it's a change to holiday plans or something new for dinner. Change rocks the Lime world because they can't guarantee their own safety. What will happen? What's new that I can't do? Introduce ideas gently with as much notice as possible and leave time for them to get used to the idea. Ultimately, prove to them that this is a safe decision and that when they agree, they won't be embarrassed in any way and you will support them.

Slow down and quieten down. Adjust the pace and turn down the volume. When you ask a Lime a question, give them the space and time to answer. Don't jump into the space because you think they're taking too long to answer. Wait, because they're still thinking!

Pay attention. Limes can keep their feelings very much to themselves, which can be a negative when they're angry, frustrated, or upset. Create an environment that makes it easier for Limes to talk about their feelings. Watch carefully for the sensitive Lime's changing moods, so you can help them.

Don't invade. *Limes are creatures* of habit with a natural progression from liking routine and order. Limes value the past. Their pleasant memories consist of things that ran smoothly. Routine provides comfort in troubled times. However, Limes don't want a big hug when things get a little rocky. They want to be left alone to think and reflect. And when they are upset, let them have their space and let them know you're there if they need you.

How Limes See Themselves

How Limes See Themselves	How others can see Limes
efficient	anal-retentive
organised	militant
responsible	parental
careful with money	tight with money
conscientious	lacking spontaneity
dependable	boring
accurate	fussy
sensitive	high maintenance

Short and Sweet

Lime Characteristics

- neat
- organised
- cautious decision-makers
- detailed
- perfectionists
- accurate
- quick to judge
- sensitive
- creative
- responsible
- modest
- dependable
- conservative
- deep thinkers.

Spot the Lime

- neat office and house
- neat clothes
- introverted
- gestures close to body
- limited tone
- steady speech
- scrutinising eyes.

Dealing with Limes

- respect their ways
- don't threaten their safety or security
- slow down and quieten down
- pay attention
- don't invade their space.

Chapter 4

Beautiful Bananas

Banana at a Glance

Likes	Dislikes
relationships	impatience
peace	intolerance
harmony	aggression
helping others	conflict
Good bits	**Not-so-good bits**
empathic	can't say no
intuitive	avoid speaking up
caring	procrastinators
Communication	**Motivation**
talk through problems	acceptance
look for emotional depth	being needed
highly personalised	peace
give compliments easily	
empathic listeners	
avoid conflict	

Bananas are the sweetest of the bunch. Friendly and caring, you immediately warm to them. They are versatile, accepting, adaptable, **trusting**, and **empathic**. Their ability to be a shoulder to cry on is legendary. Ever sat next to someone on a plane and found yourself pouring out your problem? If they listened and nodded and patted your hand, there's a Banana right there.

In fact, Banana's superpower is empathy. Out of all the Fruit, they are the best equipped to get inside someone else's head and understand their perspective. This gives them an advantage when it comes to challenging conversations.

Bananas make great mediators. Their ability to empathise with each party and provide calm advice allows them to take part in mediation and fulfils their desire to help.

Family and relationships are of prime importance to them: nothing else comes first. They are happiest when all their relationships are in harmony, at work and at home. Bananas simple love people.

Bananas trust their initial impression of someone, pre-ferring to believe the best of people. They see good every-where. Apples, meanwhile, can't quite believe that the motives behind the Banana's desires and actions are simply as pure as they are.

Bananas have a finely tuned sense of intuition. Sensitive creatures themselves, they're the first to be aware of others' body language or facial expressions when something is wrong. It goes without saying that these people can make great loyal partners and friends.

They're happy to be in the background, with no desire to take centre stage, and will take instruction as long as it sits well with their values. This doesn't mean that Bananas can't be good leaders, but their easy going way of processing and time often prevents them from being in the front seat. However, once a Banana gets to a leadership position, they can be very strong indeed. Because of their wonderful ability to connect with people and their lack of criticism and pressure, their team will follow them to the ends of the earth. And smart Bananas have other Fruit around them that complement the areas where they're not as strong.

A Banana is a laidback piece of Fruit. They are excellent at going with the flow and don't stress easily because they try not to put themselves in stressful situations. They're not natural goal-setters, because this creates high expectations, which can cause stress. Without high expectations, a Banana can go about life peacefully.

As low risk takers, Bananas stay out of trouble.

Banana Joe once told me that if he didn't take any risks, he couldn't get hurt. While it has kept him safe, it's also created feelings of inadequacy and insignificance because he feels he has no great achievements and hasn't allowed himself to be heard.

Bananas are not naturally proactive. They will often hold back until asked and hate to be seen as pushy. If it involves helping people, Bananas can make quicker decisions. With anything else, they tend to procrastinate because their care factor is low or they really don't mind. Deciding on car insurance: low care factor. Deciding on which movie to see: really don't mind.

They sometimes end up in sales roles because they are "people" people, but if this requires them to prospect and cold call, they often fall short of their targets. They're talented at relationship building, but their fear of losing the relationship can cost them sales.

Bananas don't function in the extremes of life, but are happy to walk the middle road, not causing trouble. No impulsive

Mango holidays that nobody can afford, no Lime sitting on a nest-egg and never doing anything. They're somewhere safely in between. They are unlikely to ever suffer the stress-related illnesses that Apples can so easily bring on themselves. They're chilled and take everything at a steady pace. When faced with a crisis, they're likely to take time out for a cup of tea and a good lie down while they think about it ... and think about it. Bananas are procrastinators by nature and pretty relaxed about time. They know that if they wait long enough, someone else will fix the problem or make the decision.

At a conference, I noticed a jacket left on a chair when the room cleared. I took it to lunch to find its owner, who was happily slouched in the lounge having a drink. He smiled, thanked me, and said, 'I knew someone would bring it to me eventually.' You see? Not much worry or stress in Banana world. Unlike the Limes who procrastinate because conditions must be perfect before they act, the Banana often procrastinates because they really don't want to do it.

If there is a stress factor in a Banana's life, it comes from their feelings around guilt. Guilt is a natural part of their make-up and, because of their desire to help and please, often a default setting when something goes wrong. *Was it my fault?* is the first thing a Banana wonders. They take on unnecessary guilt—for bad weather when an overseas friend visits, for their partner's behaviour, for not being able to meet at a time someone else wants, or when a relationship breaks down and they think they could have helped.

Bananas are givers. It's essential for them, and to be in a caring role gives them purpose. Lucky us.

One downside to the Banana's keenness to help is the trouble they have saying no to anything. Imagine how easy it is to take advantage of this well-meaning and soft Fruit. Bananas' favourite phrases are: whatever you think; I don't mind; whatever you want. Bananas will say "yes" when they really want to say "no". They think they can fit in that one extra report, or manage to pick up someone else's kids after school, but because they say yes to everything, they end up being too busy and they are not able to do what they said they would. The very thing the Banana wanted, to help and be liked, backfires.

If you really care about what a Banana wants or thinks, you're going to need patience to coax the information out of them. They often avoid what they see as trouble by not speaking up. But this sweet Fruit can be highly emotional which can express itself in tears of upset or anger. The danger is that every time they don't speak up for what they really want, they build resentment and anger inside. This hard little tumour grows and eats away at the outwardly-content Banana until it threatens to burst. It may take a month, it may take years, but these are the Bananas who suddenly walk out of marriages, leaving behind a dazed partner who shakes their head and asks, 'What happened?'

Bananas hate pressure. You'll face a tough call if you try to pressure a Banana into doing something. You're likely to hit an impenetrable brick wall. It's far better to go slowly and show them the benefits to the people involved. Frustrating for some, but better results long-term.

Another common Banana trait is their absolute dread of any sort of confrontation. They will avoid it at all costs. If someone jumps the queue on a Banana, they'll shrug and let them in. *What can I do?* their eyes ask the other customers. Their meal arrives and it's not the right one. *Ah, well, why cause a fuss? It will do.* If someone is spreading rumours about them at work, those rumours continue to spread, because the Banana isn't likely to initiate a confrontation. They have low energy levels with their laidback attitude, so they'd rather take the pain than risk a conflict and use up much-needed energy.

Bananas can even get upset if they witness confrontation in others. Raised voices and sharp words cause consternation in Banana world. Can you imagine the difference between Bananas and Apples? The Fruit who get pleasure from a heated verbal sparring? Is it any wonder we have difficulty understanding each other?

One Banana girl told me that seeing two people argue, even if she doesn't know them and she's not involved, can make her cry. This doesn't mean it's a weakness, Apples. But it does mean they react differently to you.

It's no surprise what I like best in Bananas. Their wonderful, warm personalities make you feel valued and welcomed, especially in a new group. They are kind and patient and caring. Lovely.

Spot the Banana

Bananas make you feel comfortable, like a warm doona on a cold night. They're the first to offer you a cup of tea or a beer. Bananas listen with empathy, their eyes are soft and caring. Of all the Fruit, it's easiest for the Banana to mirror your own body language in an effort to get on. They can also be touchy-feely and quite comfortable inside your personal space.

You'll find their clothes casual and conforming, and a Banana desk will be an endearing mess as they lack structure and are often undisciplined. They're also the most likely to have a range of photos of family and friends and keep every soft toy or promotional item they've ever been given.

When Bananas speak, they have a genial, steady tone, use a limited vocal range, and can talk a lot about people and relationships. Although they're non-threatening and inoffensive, if you're working with a Banana, you may find their endless chatter frustrating and unfocused.

The Banana's demeanour is always respectful, but the biggest hint to a Banana personality is their desire to oblige and do whatever everyone else wants. They'll offer to go first, last, or whatever makes life easier for everyone else involved. They'll meet you at the place of your choosing, go to your choice of movie, and have lamb for dinner because you feel like it. They will always stop and find time for you, no matter how busy they are.

So how do I deal with Bananas?

It's all about relationships—appreciate the four things the Banana most values:

- harmonious relationships
- time with the people they care about
- the opportunity to help
- a peaceful life.

To connect with a Banana, keep these core values of peace and relationships in mind.

Don't pressure them, motivate them. Bananas can be frustrating for the other Fruit, with their easygoing style and lack of urgency or apparent enthusiasm. But you won't get anywhere by raising your voice, being impatient, and making demands. This attitude sends Bananas into hiding; they hate pressure of any sort. That said, Bananas do need motivation from external sources as this is not one of their strong points. Trust is critical. They are looking for the values they respect such as empathy, care, and compassion. Once you build this trust, Bananas will be loyal and dedicated partners.

Listen to them. Don't be impatient. Listen with your left and right brain for what's being said and what's being felt. Then get them involved. This shows you have respected them by listening. Bananas like to be part of the solution. When you're giving information, remember that Bananas need a user-friendly experience. If you use too many statistics, their eyes will quickly glaze over.

Create a safe environment for honest communication. Bananas look for openness, honesty, and patience in a trusting environment. They're often reluctant to share their opinion for fear of confrontation, even at home. To establish better Banana communication, you have to help draw information from them, so you need to create an environment where they feel they can approach you without fear. Once you know their thoughts, you can encourage them to speak up and help them to make decisions.

Be respectful. Be firm without being aggressive. Respect their emotions, but don't pander to them. Be patient; they don't think quickly or decisively, but that doesn't mean they don't think.

How Bananas See Themselves

How Bananas see themselves	How others can see Bananas
accommodating	indecisive
caring	overly sentimental
inoffensive	spineless
empathic	irritating
friendly	chatterbox
easygoing	weak
sensitive	overly emotional
loyal	clingy

Short and Sweet

Banana Characteristics

- intuitive
- loyal
- team players
- patient
- inoffensive
- easy going
- guilt-ridden
- low risk-takers
- procrastinators
- laidback
- can't say no
- accommodating
- love a chat
- don't like confrontation or pressure.

Spot the Banana

- touchy-feely—in your space
- casually dressed
- messy space
- steady tone
- lots of chatter
- obliging
- warm energy.

Dealing with the Banana

- don't pressure them: motivate them
- take time to build the relationship
- listen to them
- create a safe environment for honest communication
- be respectful.

Chapter 5

Fruity Blends

We have looked at the extreme versions of pure Fruit, those who exhibit traits on a 9/10 scale rather than a 2/10. We do this because it's the most memorable way to provide a sharp picture of traits peculiar to each Fruit. It helps to recognise the different traits and manage them more easily. Unless you are "off the planet" strong in one Fruit, you will have recognised yourself in some of the others.

The danger of restricting people to the confines of their Fruit box is that we're labelling them as 100% pure. We're all incredibly complex human beings and no-one is just one Fruit. Every one of us is a Fruit Salad. Learning about different Fruit in a simple and fun way helps us to recognise elements in ourselves and others and use the knowledge as a guideline for more effective behaviour.

The idea of pop psychology is to break down behaviour into easily digestible chunks. Some of us are strong (more than 35%) in one segment. Some of us will be strong across two, some even across three or perhaps across all four. People can become confused when they have identified their top preference and make the mistake of thinking that is the sum total of their traits:

I'm an Apple but I can't make quick decisions.

I'm a Mango but I hate public speaking.

I'm a Lime but I love people.

I'm a Banana but I don't mind conflict.

If we only think in terms of pure Apple, Mango, Lime, or Banana, it's easy to be confused. In this section, we dive deeper to consider our blends and in particular, our top two preferences. These are the preferences we default to, especially under pressure. However, it's also critical to remember this: we are all capable of donning any of the Fruit hats.

The sweetest, kindest Banana will become a hard-core Apple when defending her child. The Lime, terrified of public speaking, will step up to the plate to deliver a beautiful eulogy for a loved one. We have natural attributes which come easily but that doesn't mean that we can't learn the skills of the other Fruit. To learn to be kind, to speak up, to have more discipline, to be more flexible. It just takes more energy to work in the areas that don't come naturally.

Who Are You Hanging Out With?

Some people tell me their behaviour is the same at work as at home. Others tell me they are the opposite. That's because both environments are defined by the people in them.

The way your Fruit plays out is also linked to your type of partner, especially when you have a shared Fruit style.

If you're an Apple/Lime and are required to call on your attributes of organisational skills and decision-making in the workplace then go home to your Mango/Banana partner, you will play the same role and use the same skills. This is because all bases are covered between your Fruit combinations. It's nicely balanced.

Conversely, you may go home to your Apple/Banana partner who takes over the Apple role and allows you to melt into your quieter and calmer Lime space. If your partner is particularly challenged in one area, you may find yourself increasing your second or even third preference.

Let's take a look at our top blends and see how this works. The four most common blends are: Apple/Lime, Mango/Banana, Apple/Mango, and Lime/Banana. The two blends created by the diagonals are Mango/Lime and Apple/Banana.

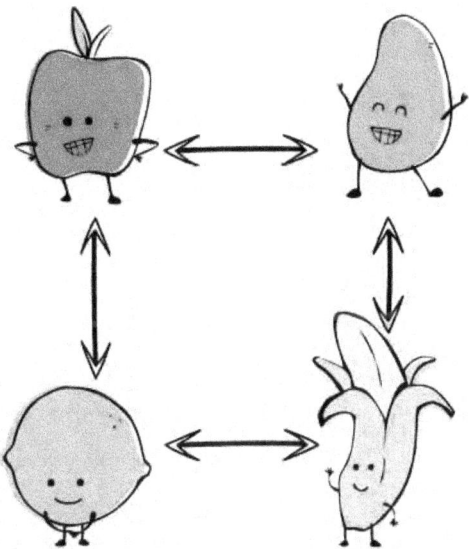

Diagram 2: Common Top Two Blends

The higher your score in these top two blends, the stronger those traits will be. If your top two blends are more than 65% of your score, consider it a super blend.

Over the last twenty years, thousands of people have completed the Ripe Fruit Personality Profile, either through my conference keynotes, live workshops, video training, or virtual workshops. Of those, around 30% report acting in the same way at work as they do at home. These people are usually more extreme versions of each Fruit. But even for them, different circumstances can expose a different Fruit. Ultimately, all of us have the potential to develop any traits from the four Fruit. It's just that our natural preference comes so much more easily. Each one of us has a slice of everything and different circumstances or certain people can bring out our inner Fruit salad.

Let's take a closer look.

Natural Blends

Apple/Lime

This natural blend is the super left brainer. You are extremely logical and task driven. The Apple gathers hard data and the Lime analyses it before any decision is made. To consider making a decision in any other way is incomprehensible. The Apple enjoys conceptual thinking and the Lime likes to make sure the detail is 100% correct. The Apple wants to make a quick decision, but the Lime needs to make sure the decision is the right one so undertakes all the research.

The Apple quite likes conflict, but the Lime doesn't like speaking up. The Apple thinks big picture, but the Lime won't take a risk unless it's carefully thought out. The Lime demands perfection and the Apple expects his children enter every competition and win. The Apple is an extrovert, the Lime is an introvert. These are just a taste of many ways your Apple/Lime may play out.

This blend is quite natural because it crosses over in many areas.

Apples and Limes:

- are realistic
- are pragmatic
- find it difficult to relate to intuition
- have zero tolerance for laziness
- have zero tolerance for stupidity
- are good at meeting deadlines
- like task and process
- have integrity to keep commitments
- struggle to place the same value as right brainers on emotions
- set themselves and others a high bar
- won't give up
- fear losing financial control.

When you're with a Mango or Banana, watch out for these areas:

You are the Fun Police; the grown up

The Apple/Lime blend can take on a critical parent role in a relationship, setting the rules, knowing what's best. They may be excellent at planning and achieving results, but less focused on their partner's needs, who can end up feeling like a scolded child. In our linear business world, the Apple/Lime blends typically find themselves in a leadership role at work and are often content to continue this role at home. It works with their desire for control and perfection.

Problem solving

Yes, you are good at it, but you want to ask a million questions to get to the bottom of what went wrong. And perhaps all your partner needs is a hug and a glass of wine.

Socialising

You already have to deal with imbeciles at work, why do you have to go to that barbeque where more idiots hang out? Because your partner needs to get out more than you do.

Emotions

You struggle to show them, and at times, share them. Having lower preferences in the right brain means you may become detached from the emotional impact of your decisions. But if you are with a Mango, Banana, or blend of the two, you may find yourself creating a whole world of pain and hurt for them, even if it is unintentional on your part.

Insight

An Apple/Lime friend told me that he once cut off someone who could have been the love of his life. They live in different countries and he had pursued and exhausted all avenues of being together. He is not without emotion and told me it hurt but it was the only logical decision to make.

The best bit

You will always look after your family financially. They will never have to worry.

Mango/Banana

This double right-brained blend is skilled in making people feel comfortable, understanding emotions, and creating diplomatic solutions. They often leave the corporate world to establish their own business. Fuelled by the Mango desire to make a difference and the Banana desire to serve, unfortunately, if they're light on the left-brained side which includes a keen eye for accounts and budgets, this blend will struggle to succeed.

Your decisions are based on intuition and the people involved. While this can work, you risk making a poor decision if you constantly ignore logic. This can be super frustrating if you have a left-brained partner and earn their scorn for being soft.

The Mango loves being the centre of attention at a party, but the Banana is terrified of public speaking. The Mango can talk non-stop, but the Banana won't face conflict. The Mango loves the idea of fabulous holidays, but the Banana really hopes someone else will plan them. These are just some of the ways that the Mango/Banana plays out. This too is a complementary blend combining both right-brained Fruit which cross over in many areas. Mangoes and Bananas:

- love people and relationships
- talk a lot
- want everybody to have fun
- live in the moment
- are not driven by money, but a need to feel happy
- want to change the world either in a big way or by serving others.

Here's how you may drive your opposite partner crazy:

Problem solving

Your problem-solving technique is of using your instinct without logic. Say no more.

You talk too much

Mango stories are funny to a point but when is exaggeration a lie? Bananas talk about people all the time and the endless chatter causes your partner to tune out at best or cut you off at worst.

You're messy

Physically and mentally. Let's face it, organisation is not your thing. Prepare to be scolded for not being tidy, or thinking ahead, or not thinking at all.

You're not that great with time

Don't leave your partner sitting in the car with the engine running for fifteen minutes while you do that last-minute wash or try to find your sunglasses.

Insight

I lived alternate weeks in two cities for thirteen years because I wouldn't let go of either my children or my new love. Only Banana love and Mango belief that anything is possible could make that work. Or stupidity.

The best bit

You bring joy, fun, optimism, and love to the relationship. Never let it go.

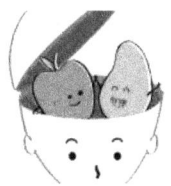

Mango/Apple

The Apple/Mango is the most intense blend and exhausting to be around, as they move at a fast pace, juggling several balls at once, which are usually not related. There is no sitting around. It's all action, although not often around structure or rules.

Many successful entrepreneurs have an Apple/Mango profile, combining Mango flair and risk with Apple intellect and analysis. This is a big-picture conceptual blend with no desire for detail or what they see as the mundane in life. The Mango comes up with the vision and the Apple backs it up with logic.

Believing that appearances are of the utmost importance, this blend takes great care to create an impeccable image. The personable Mango will be interested and focused on you in the moment, but underneath the Apple never stops planning the next game. If the Mango is the predominant Fruit, others can mistakenly think they have got an easy catch, only to get caught by the smiling assassin, the Apple.

This blend shares the following traits:

- extroversion
- optimism
- big picture thinking
- seeing the full perspective
- fast-paced thinking
- love a challenge
- outspokenness
- do not let opposition stop them in their drive
- resilience.

Here's what to look out for in the relationship with your Limes and Bananas.

You're exhausting

Slow down, take a breath, or lock yourself away. You can't wake up and start talking business strategy before you get out of bed.

Detail

You're bad at it. Make sure if you're planning that surprise birthday weekend for your partner you've got the detail covered. By the same token, don't let your partner end up with all the grunt work because you only do "big picture". I have an Apple/Mango friend who is exceptional at charming people into doing work for nothing. They are content just to be in her orbit, and she is content to accept their adoration and their work.

Nobody can compete with you

You do things first and you do them better. While your partner is thinking about joining a tennis club, you have signed up and are already playing a better game than them. This can manifest itself in low self-esteem and feelings of inferiority for your partner. You must have new challenges and adventures all the time because you are more self-absorbed than most and get on with living your life. Independent relationships are healthy but be careful your partner does not feel left behind and left out.

Insight

An Apple/Mango friend told me that if she was heading to a job (she earns a living as a professional speaker) with her husband, and he was hit by a car as they crossed the road, she would still go to the gig. But she would call an ambulance first.

The best bit

In a relationship, you're the doer. The person who plans and is full of big, exciting things and then makes sure they happen.

Banana/Lime

The Banana/Lime blend is a lovely fit: calm more often than not and moving at a steady pace. Limes and Bananas share the traits of highly valuing family, peace, and harmony, so this common blend doesn't face as much confusion as other blends might.

But there are differences. The Lime is a natural worrier, the Banana is easy going. The Lime is neat and organised, the Banana is a little loose. The Lime is anxious around change and the Banana is chilled. It works, because the easy going Banana is happy to go with whatever the Lime decides as long as nobody is getting hurt in the process.

This blend shares the following traits:

- a love of family
- steady thinkers
- values stability
- dislikes show offs
- sensitivity
- doesn't want to be centre stage
- dislikes confrontation
- likes detail, one in facts, the other in feelings

- introverted
- both romantics, albeit at different levels.

Challenges this blend brings to a relationship with their opposites are:

Lack of assertiveness

When confronted with the dominating Apples and Mangoes, this sensitive blend chooses one of two things: not to speak up out of fear or deciding this is an issue not worth speaking up about and then facing confrontation.

The tendency to play victim

The natural Lime worry and sensitivity combined with the Banana fear of confrontation can have this blend thinking that negative situations only ever happen to them. Mango and Apple partners will have little time for this, even though the concern is very real in the Banana/Lime mind.

Procrastination and decision-making

Neither Limes nor Bananas are quick decision-makers. The Lime will go into overload with the information required to decide; the Banana will be overwhelmed with the information and mentally bin it. Too many statistics, too much detail and Banana will just shut that folder down. The result: a Lime/Banana freeze.

Insight

A romantic Banana/Lime friend was going away for a week on business. Full of love, she bought a beautiful card to tell her Mango partner exactly how much she loved him. Imagine the pleasure he would get when he read it. Unfortunately, the Mango didn't bother to check the letter box for a week, so the love became trash.

The best bit

You hold the team together. You may not think so, but you are the stabilising, steady, solid glue that keeps the house from falling down.

Slightly Weirder Blends

The last two blends are the least common and certainly the most confusing if these happen to be your top two preferences. Mango/Lime and Apple/Banana are diagonally opposite quadrants and by now you'll know they are opposite in pretty much everything. These two blends don't face the same challenges as the previous four. You might spend a lot of time feeling confused, but don't despair. There are certain advantages to these diagonal blends, apart from making you a damned interesting person.

Diagram 3: Less Common Top Two Blends

Mango/Lime

The confusion!

The Mango wants to go away for the weekend. The Lime says you can't afford it. The Lime wants to develop a detailed spreadsheet for the household budget, but the Mango wants to buy what they feel like in the moment. The Mango is eternally optimistic; the Lime is prone to negativity and pessimism. Mango is big picture; Lime is micro detail. I'm an extrovert! Oh, I forgot, I'm an introvert.

The Mango-Lime is often exhausted because of this ongoing battle. Decision-making will depend on which Fruit is strongest. The Mango will jump to spontaneous decisions as the Lime stresses, or the Lime will take time to carefully consider a decision while the Mango nearly has a seizure waiting.

But there is one spot where this blend crosses over. Both are creative. The Mango through their view that anything is possible, and the Lime through their innate introversion and deep thinking. Therefore, you will find a high percentage of the Lime/Mango blend on stage as actors, performers, and musicians.

It can be confusing for some to see that their quiet Lime friend is quite at home on stage rocking a wailing sax, but this apparent contradiction is quite natural. When performing, the Lime musician is wonderfully comfortable showcasing the skill they've perfected along with their Mango extroversion. As you can imagine, this can lead to a touch of neuroticism. You want the limelight, but you can't bear not to be perfect, so you agonise, worry, and lose sleep. Or the Mango jumps in and agrees to something then the Lime panics. You agreed to what?

The more likely scenario is the Mango will have a brilliant idea, often accompanied by a glass or two of wine. The next day the Lime will be trapped in procrastination in the event the idea is not good enough. You can be the life of the party who, behind closed doors, can disappear into dark, solo thoughts. If you are strong in one quadrant, these traits will dominate. It's when your Mango and Lime are quite even that you will struggle the most.

Challenges

This blend's challenges in a relationship are based primarily around their own opposing views and internal battles.

You need a partner who understands this apparent conflict in your personality because you are probably the most emotional blend of all the Fruit. Mango loves drama and is prone to theatrics, loving life not only when it's good but also when things go wrong. There is a certain excitement that stirs the Mango's heart. Combine this, however, with the Lime propensity to worry about things that may not ever happen, or to lose sleep for weeks on something that has.

This can play out in a troubling way. The Mango desire for variety and fun can lead to extra hard partying with recreational drugs and alcohol. As these are natural depressants, they act to exacerbate a Lime's natural anxiety. It's a difficult cycle which requires an empathic and patient partner. Mango's feelings of self-doubt and desire to be liked sends them out to meet people, but before long, the Lime is desperate for alone time, leading to exhaustion and often long periods of gloominess.

Mango looseness plays agony with the Lime desire for perfection, and Lime obsessive behaviour will have Mango turning themselves inside out. All these internal struggles are debilitating before the Mango/Lime even begins to work on their relationship. You may be more complicated than most, but the same principles apply. Know yourself, understand your quirks, and realise this is completely normal for you. Recognise when your behaviour may be creating obstacles and reach for help by opening your own Apple and Banana files, or through the love of your understanding partner.

Insight

A Mango/Lime told me she had planned a huge garden party for her fortieth birthday a few months out. She was excited about the planning and her Mango had the vision of roses in bloom, a beautiful wisteria covered arbour, delicious platters of food, with everyone wearing pink and white. Her parents were coming from interstate. Everything would be wonderful.

As the time edged closer, her Lime woke up. *What the hell were you thinking? This will never work! I don't want to be with people anyway. What if it rains? I don't want to be forty!* She cancelled the party and fell into a depressed state for weeks because she felt she had let everybody down.

The Best Bit

You are bloody interesting.

If you can accept you are made up of often opposing views, you can see life in a very balanced way. If this is you, you are getting two different perspectives on everything, allowing you to think both logically and emotionally. This is a gift! Enjoy your Lime's careful decision-making and ordered process combined with your Mango's optimism and ability to connect and inspire people. An impressive combination.

Apple/Banana

And if you think the Mango/Limes are confused, these guys take the Fruit cake.

Banana wants to rest; Apple wants to drive forward. Apple wants to debate; Banana wants to retreat. Apple wants to sack a worker; Banana wants to provide counselling.

No wonder you are conflicted. There is nothing in this blend that crosses over. Nothing. Nil. Nada.

It's even more confusing for the rest of us. Just when you think you've got this people-watching thing nailed, along comes an Apple/Banana. If you meet them socially, you may think they are lovely, warm, generous, genuine, and interested in you and your life. Yet you hear from their partner that they are immovable in their arguments and rule the home with an iron fist.

You're perfectly normal for this profile, but you will never see things as clearly as a stronger version of just one Fruit or a combination in one hemisphere. If you can get your head around this contradiction, you'll find the foundation to develop great strengths. When making decisions, the Apple will gather the hard data and the Banana will weigh up the human impact before you go ahead.

So, what does this mean for your relationship? Because we are all unique, each relationship is different and dependent on two things: firstly, the strength of the blend in each person, and secondly, whether you are with your complete opposite, or you have a cross over blend between you.

Challenges

How this works in your relationship will depend on the strength of your Fruit and who you are with. If you are especially strong in either your Apple or Banana, that Fruit will dominate. But like the Mango/Lime, if you are even across the two, the issue is one of confusion and conflict. However, unlike the Mango/Lime, this blend is not as emotional, because the clout of the Apple won't tolerate time wasted on emotions and worry. Who will be out today? Apple Crush or Banana Smoothie?

Typically the issue with this blend is that your partner will be lulled into the semi false security of being with an all-giving, all-loving Banana, and the first time real conflict arises the Apple bites, often sending your partner into shock. Your test then is to manage those extremes.

Insight

A decade ago, I made a new friend. Abigail was delightful, interested in me and my life, offering to help whenever she could. Charming, easy company, we shared a lot of laughs.

One day I made what I thought was a hilarious comment designed to get a laugh, comparing Abigail to a celebrity who was less than attractive and smart. Suddenly Abigail's Banana shut down, the Apple emerged, and I received a bollocking that shocked me to the core. I am now careful never to wake the dragon.

The Best Bit

Like the Mango/Lime, if you can compartmentalise and understand your strengths, you are awesome. You have the Apple ability to make fast, informed decisions, get results and see the big picture, combined with Banana intuition, compassion, and a genuine desire to help and to serve. Apple/Bananas can make incredible parents and leaders.

Peas in a Pod

The fun and games start when you and your partner have the same predominant Fruit. This will explain why you may change personalities between your work environment and your home. The key to success is awareness and respect, for yourself and for your partner, as you may need to shift to your second or third preference.

Two Apples

You're the Power Couple at school drop off, having risen early to manage emails and social media, exercise, sort the kids, and paint the house if you have half a chance. The danger is your work is so stimulating that your risk doing little else.

Let's say you are Apple/Mango and your partner is an Apple/Lime
Everybody wants to be in charge. The Apple in you wants and needs control. So does the Apple in your partner. You win because your blend is louder and more extroverted. Their Lime will emerge more at home because that's the bit that's missing from your blend; no one else is keeping law and order. They will look after the detail for you.

Your partner is an Apple/Banana
Easy, you win again on the control piece—a big, dominant, pushy thing that you are. Your partner brings the nurturing and care to the house and looks after the daily grind that you

don't want to. They ensure you have sincere friends and some down time to recharge.

Your partner is Apple/Mango
Someone needs to look after the detail of the household so one of you will reach into their third or even fourth preference and find their inner Lime and Banana.

Two Mangoes

This is a party house! Their desire to be liked means they will do whatever they must to be popular. Their generosity ensures they have lots of friends. Together they learn to bounce off one another so they become a two-person comedy act as the stories become funnier.

You're a Mango/Banana and your partner is a Mango/Lime
It can't be a party all of the time. Your partner will have to forgo their Mango sometimes because their Lime will inevitably end up being the sensible one who looks after the money and watches the spending. It also means they will probably do all the worrying. They may not want that role, preferring their Mango side, but circumstances create the necessity. The Mango/Banana is happy not having to do detail or worry, because their partner now does it all for them.

Your partner is a Mango/Apple
Same thing. Here your partner's Mango will have to be put on hold because someone needs to be the grown up in this house. At home, their Apple will dominate, possibly making you feel quite foolish at times, but keeping spending and frivolity in line.

Your partner is a Mango/Banana
May the gods help you. Get a good accountant.

Two Limes

You are a quiet, intellectual, and feeling couple. Your house is ordered. It is not rushed. There is reason behind everything. There is routine and security. If anything, you'll need lessons in robust debate, because you're both prone to withdraw into moodiness rather than confront.

You're a Lime/Banana and your partner is a Lime/Apple
Okay, so your house is organised, clean and tidy. No arguments there. And your second preferences are perfectly complementary. The Banana in you makes sure there's plenty of love to go around and the Apple steps in to make the hard decisions when the two Limes overthink.

Your partner is a Lime/Mango
A nice combination. The house will be tidy, but you'll have plenty of time put aside for fun and relaxation, once all the chores are done and the list has been ticked off.

Your partner is a Lime/Banana
You have a lot in common and will argue little. But sometimes the quiet life and the agonisingly careful decisions will annoy the third and fourth preferences and one of the fast thinking, big picture traits will emerge from one of you to push everyone on a bit.

Two Bananas

Yours is a chilled-out house where everyone gets along with no arguing allowed. There's no pretension. Relaxed and accommodating is your motto with no rush to get anything done to deadline.

You are a Banana/Apple and your partner is a Banana/Lime
The two Bananas will just want to hang out and chill all the time but neither of your second preferences will let you. The Lime will analyse all potential problems, Apple will ensure the right decisions are being made and together work is being done.

Your partner is a Banana/Mango
Your Apple will appear more and more as your right-brained partner wants to chill or party, volunteer at the school, and look after people around them. Someone needs to take control, so your natural preference will take a back seat at home.

Your partner is a Banana/Apple
It is a confused but formidable household. Goals and results. Charity balls. Down time and drive. At least there is understanding of each other's constant inner conflict and confusion.

Although we tend to work in our top two preferences, we do of course, at times, access all four quadrants when called for. Imagine you don't have a partner to pick up the slack for you. That's perfectly fine because this wonderful tangle of traits is all within you, should you choose to use them. You may find it takes unusual situations to take you out of your comfort zone.

The Apple/Lime calls on Mango and Banana when, as mother of the bride, they must make everyone feel comfortable and welcome at their daughter's wedding.

The Mango/Banana can access their Apple and Lime when planning their complex wills across a variety of children, stepchildren, and charities.

The Apple/Mango can harness their inner Lime and Banana when faced with the bedside vigil beside a dying parent.

The Lime/Banana can find their inner Apple and Mango to plan early stages of building a house.

The Mango/Lime is capable of finding their inner Apple at the funeral of a close friend, when total control is required because the family is devastated. And you will find your inner Banana to care for them.

The Apple/Banana can dip into their Mango when faced with an important social event that will mean the difference between getting a job or not. And you will find your inner Lime when the same company tests you on the details of a balance sheet.

We are all capable of connecting with our third and fourth preferences, but be warned, it does take a little more energy to work in a quadrant that doesn't come naturally. You may be exhausted, but it can also feel hugely liberating to go somewhere you haven't been before.

Can we change our Fruit preference?

As adults, you will always retain the essence of who you are but there are five main factors that can lead to exposing and developing the different Fruit within:

1. your partner at home
2. your family life
3. being out of your comfort zone
4. your age
5. your work culture.

Your partner

As mentioned above, your partner's personality can affect which Fruit you bring out at home, especially if your first preference is the same Fruit. You may find yourself working more in your second or third preference.

For example, if one of you is a Mango/Lime and the other is a Mango/Banana, your relationship has a lot of right brain activity. The Mango/Lime will inevitably end up being the sensible one who looks after the money and watches the spending, drawing on their Lime side. It also means they will probably do all the worrying. They may not want that role, preferring their Mango side, but circumstances create the necessity. The Mango/Banana is happy to be spared from detail and worry, because their partner now does it all for them.

This can be draining for the person forced to spend all their time in a secondary mode. Not being permitted to use their natural preference can create frustration and resentment.

The antidote is awareness, both of yourself and your partner. Know yourself.

Take an Apple/Mango and an Apple/Lime. The Apple in you knows your wants, and needs to be in control, and being the stronger Apple, you've taken it. How does your Apple partner feel? Whether it's management of the financials or lack of control in family decisions, put the topic out on the table and talk about it.

Approach the challenge from a loving standpoint and find a compromise. Never let frustration and resentment simmer for long or it will boil over. When that happens, it's way too hard to scrub clean.

Your family

The working Banana is keen, eager to please, and happy to fit in with her Mango colleagues. She is married to another Banana with very strong Banana traits. They have three children, which forces this Banana mum to take control, bringing out her organisational Lime or even controlling Apple. At home, she's in charge of her domain. At work, they wouldn't recognise her.

By necessity, parenting brings out the Lime and Apple in all of us. When you need to juggle pick-ups and drop-offs for netball, dance, debating, football, swimming, and flute lessons, you'll be grateful for your inner Lime. And someone must be the boss at home, so bring out that inner Apple. And whether you're fighting it or not, parenting brings out your inner Banana. Apples will never think they can love like a Banana until they've had a child.

Out of your comfort zone

Have you ever been in a situation where you've behaved in a way that seems totally out of character? This typically happens when you find yourself somewhere that you wouldn't usually be.

A normally shy Lime is reluctantly dragged out of an audience to come up on stage and discovers they are the funniest or the best dancer. And weirdly, they enjoy it. Your child is being bullied at school and the normally calm, patient Banana becomes a demanding, immovable Apple. A Mango is asked to speak at the funeral of a close friend. They park their flippant, entertaining side to be sombre, respectful, and thoughtful. An Apple has a critical work meeting when their child is taken ill. Work takes second place. When challenging situations occur suddenly, taking us out of our comfort zone, we sometimes react in a way that can surprise us, exposing a slice of under-used Fruit.

And, in case you're wondering, alcohol makes everyone a Mango.

Age

I've noticed that as people grow older, something odd starts to happen. Primarily between fifty and sixty, they begin to morph into their diagonal opposites. I've questioned a cross-section of people in this age group from a range of industries and it appears to be quite common. Apples become tired of being the hard-nosed task master all their lives and begin to relax and bring out their inner Banana. Mangoes no longer want to be crazy Uncle Marty and decide that they wouldn't mind some money in the bank and some funds to retire on. Limes, after a lifetime of being the sensible, responsible Fruit, decide they would like to channel their inner Mango and cycle across Vietnam. And Bananas end up with nothing left to give, decide it's their turn to do some taking, and voilà, out comes their inner Apple.

Within each of us dwell the seeds of all the Fruit, waiting patiently until they are needed. Ultimately, we can bring out any Fruit if we choose to work on the traits that define it. Often those traits, because they don't come naturally, may take a little longer to master.

Work culture

In the Western business world, we lean heavily on the left brain: a world ruled by retail, oil and gas, and automotive, which prefer structure, rules, and strong decision-makers. For many right-brainers, whose preference may be people, creativity, and emotions, in order to be taken seriously and move up the corporate ladder, they must learn to bring out their inner Apple and inner Lime in the workplace. Increasingly, start-ups and technology companies have given employees the chance to bring out their inner Mango/ Banana, encouraging more playfulness and innovation within a more flexible culture.

If you act differently in the workplace, it's because the culture or nature of the work dictates. A job full of red tape and detail can bring a Mango into line. A hip marketing agency can bring out the zing in a Lime. A creative design school can make even an Apple chill a little, and a fast-paced call centre can bring out the urgency in a Banana. Remember your profile: you may have a natural preference, but we are all a delicious blend of Fruit we can access and develop whichever traits are required.

PART TWO

FRUIT PAIRINGS

Love is a fruit in season at all times, and within reach of every hand.

—Mother Theresa

Chapter 6

A Word on Fruit Combos

I t's a funny thing. When we choose our romantic partners, we often unconsciously choose our diagonal Fruit, that is an Apple with a Banana, or a Mango with a Lime, which makes sense, following the adage that opposites attract.

Psychologist and psychiatrist Carl Jung[6] popularised the idea by theorising that we're unconsciously drawn to those who exhibit qualities we find underdeveloped in our own psyches and that we seek to complete or balance ourselves through intimate attachments.

It is certainly common to pair up with our opposites. The Lime handles the family budget and makes sure we live in relative order. The Mango plans the fun stuff and leaves the detail to the Lime. Or, the Lime handles the family budget and gets frustrated that the Mango can't keep to one. The Mango plans the big reno and is frustrated when the Lime keeps stifling their big ideas.

But any couple, any Fruit, can make a relationship work. It just depends on how much you want it. Because one thing's

---

[6] Jung C, 1954, *Archetypes and the Collective Unconscious, The Collected Works of CG Jung*, translated by RFC Hull, Bollinger Series, Princeton Press, USA.

for sure, there are no perfect couples, no matter how much they may seem to be.

But how do we pick each other?

Apples like other Apples who value intelligent debate, Bananas who are thoughtful, Limes who maintain order, and Mangoes who seize opportunities.

Mangoes like Mangoes who join in the fun, Bananas who worship them, Limes who plan the activities, and Apples who get things done.

Limes like Limes who respect the rules, Mangoes who bring adventure to their lives, Bananas who co-operate, and Apples who have a sense of responsibility.

Bananas like other Bananas who return they love the way they want it, Limes who respect their feelings, Apples who take control of the hard stuff, and Mangoes who encourage them to step outside their comfort zone.

There's a plus to being with someone similar. Thinking and communicating the same way can create stability and less friction. But common language and common activities can also allow predictability and boredom to fester.

When we meet the same Fruit as ourselves, we feel a sense of relief. Finally, someone who understands me, who doesn't nag because I am too controlling/impulsive/rigid/casual. But when we meet someone unlike ourselves, an exciting voyage of discovery follows. Apples take us mountain bike riding, Mangoes introduce us to a social whirl, Limes make us feel more stable and peaceful, and Bananas love us like there's no tomorrow. Often the more dominant personality will start introducing their world. You may enjoy some activities and fake enjoyment of some, but ultimately you need to be you.

And that's when the fun begins. We fall in love attracted by our differences but then try and clone our partners into ourselves. The challenge is how to transition lustful infatuation into a profound, rich sweetness that endures.

The answer lies in self-awareness and empathy for our partner. You'll never change them. You can only change yourself.

We have more in common than you think.

We all search for someone unlike ourselves, then pull out all stops trying to change them to our reality. We live in our own micro-worlds, seeing life through our own lenses, convinced our reality is the right one.

We all procrastinate around the things we don't like to do. Apples procrastinate around the touchy-feely stuff and dealing with interpersonal problems. Mangoes procrastinate around getting organised or spending time alone to reflect. Limes procrastinate around relaxing or anything that stops the job getting done to perfection. Bananas procrastinate around negative issues such as delivering bad news or confrontation. We all allow our worst traits to escape at home, because we expect the people who love us will tolerate anything and forgive our flaws. I mean, why can't they be just like us; perfect? Our job is to correct those flaws and make them behave more like us. So that'll work. Not.

All of us feel natural resentment if we are bullied or nagged into forcing a change we don't want. All of us will clash over money and children. All of us expect to be loved in the way we live it out. An Apple may show love by being a good provider, a Mango by buying an expensive gift, a Lime by saving money, and a Banana by cooking your favourite meal. And we're a bit miffed when our partner doesn't love us the way we want.

In the following four chapters we're going to take a look at each of the Fruit, in all of their extreme glory. Each chapter stars one Fruit, with one story. But we're going to give you four versions of the same story, depending on who the Star Fruit is with. For example, in our next chapter on Apples, you'll meet Annette, and discover how one story plays out depending on whether she is with Marty the Mango, Lucy the Lime, Basim the Banana, or fellow Apple, Archie.

I suggest you start with yourself and your partner's top preferences. Then you may want to move to you and your partner's second preferences and read how the story plays out.

Or just read the whole lot for fun.

Remember:

- You may see yourself in more than one story because we're dealing with extreme versions of our Fruit.
- We are all a blend but tend to work in our top two Fruit.
- This is pop psychology, designed to have fun and learn at the same time.

Off we go.

Chapter 7

Addicted to Apples

B eing with an Apple requires a lot of time and energy. The successful Apple partnerships I've seen involve a partner who accepts and manages the Apple in a way that no-one else can.

Apples choose their mates carefully. Once they've decided to settle down, they want to make sure you're worth spending time and money on. It's likely they've developed a wish list for a perfect partner, and when they find you, they don't care about rules or books that tell them a Banana is best for them. They will be fully committed and so should you be because you're in for the ride of your life.

The apparently unemotional Apples are fiercely protective of those they love. They're almost obsessive about home and family, and often place their partner firmly on a pedestal. They keep their private lives extremely private and until there's trust, you won't be invited beyond the front door. Family is like any other interest. It is attacked with the drive and determination to make it the very best it can be. As an outsider, you wouldn't want to threaten an Apple's family.

As natural leaders, Apples are also natural delegators. Around the home, they will only do the chores they want to do and will delegate the rest to anyone, even extending beyond the immediate family to anyone who wants to help. Apples set high benchmarks for themselves and they are singularly focused on achieving their goals. And that's usually not housework.

Here's how it goes:

'Poor Annette! She's always so busy, I don't know how she does it.'

If you're Annette's parents, you end up offering to help. You're so proud of your high-achieving daughter and she works so hard, well, it's good to help her out now and then. I know of an Annette whose parents regularly do the hard jobs like mopping floors, cleaning windows, sorting out cupboards, and scrubbing the oven. She doesn't directly delegate, but all of a sudden, those jobs belong to Mum and Dad.

UNDERSTATEMENT ALERT!

Apples do not like to be wrong and when they are wrong, they are not likely to admit it. They typically look to blame something or someone, else. This is because they can't fail. In their minds, someone else's behaviour means they did not get the desired result. Extreme Apples have trouble losing an argument because they always think they're right. At work, they may have to act a little more grown-up, but at home they're not going to budge. There's a locked drawer in the Apple's mind where the words 'I was wrong' are kept.

Here's how it goes:

'You moved the sauce bottle. That's why it wasn't packed for the picnic.'

'You put the towels in the wash so I couldn't have a shower when I wanted.'

'You're meant to be navigating me. Taking those few wrong turns has nothing to do with me.'

When Annette goes on holidays, her inner workaholic tags along. Forced to sit beside the infinity pool in a luxury resort, Annette will settle with the Apple tools of leisure: her tablet and mobile phone. She can email and watch the stock market at the same time. A dream holiday. Basim will smile fondly as he dives in the water and makes friends with the barman.

Apples find life in retirement from a career job especially difficult. Having long been defined by their profession, unstructured free time creates a gap in the schedule they must fill. When people ask what they do, they'll never say they're retired. They're far more likely to say, 'I play the stock market,' or 'I manage a property portfolio'. You can bet your bottom dollar they also run the local tipping competition.

Apples spend so much time immersed in their worlds of theories, learning, and problem-solving you may sometimes feel they're not mentally with you. While it may appear that they are distancing themselves from family life, it's more likely they simply don't notice the everyday things that bother you, like leaving a glass on the table or clothes that need folding.

An Apple's limited ability to express their feelings extends to relaxing with friends. They are most at ease when engaged in an activity—fishing, gardening, watching a play, or going to a football game. Don't ask them to discuss feelings or emotions. In the Apple's locked drawer of words, safely hidden, are 'I'm sorry,' and 'I love you.' They know those words are in the drawer, so while they may think the words, they just can't bear to unlock the drawer and put their feelings on the table. That would reveal too much and run the risk of losing control.

If you confront an Apple over this, they'll say they're just being efficient—why state the obvious?

In the workplace, Apples remain deliberately unemotional which allows them to maintain control. Instinctively, they don't trust people and consider revealing emotions to be a sign of weakness. This can extend to their personal relationships, so in the early days, even years, you may have to be patient as your Apple learns how to trust. In what seems like a contradiction, you may find out more about what's happening in your Apple partner's life when you're out with friends. That's because the Apple feels they can tell their friends what they're doing and not be accountable, as they feel they should be to you.

They hate dinnertime small talk associated with certain friends and will do their best to ensure those dinner partners are soon eliminated. Unfortunately, the Apple can't choose your friends or their partners. They disapprove of most of them anyway. If you insist on pushing your Apple partner into these situations, you'd better be prepared for some pretty blunt exchanges. Apples aren't known for their social graces.

Apples love conversations that have direction, so they enjoy planning trips and renovating houses as long as you keep it big picture. Remember, Apples find mental stimulation sexy, so start reading. They love lively sparring arguments, as long as it's all theoretical and doesn't get emotional.

They're often surprised when told they sound aggressive. They think they're being passionate and enthusiastic, but they count on the other person to fight back. Where they see a vibrant discussion, you may see an aggressive debate. Feisty as they seem, Apples find any conflict on a personal level destructive. It's not quite as enjoyable to rip apart the person you love as it is the person at the call centre. They'll still hold their ground in a personal conflict, but it's your approach, which we look at in this chapter, which will maximise your chances of success.

Watch for the competitive Apple at home. The killer instinct which allows them to be great business people can come home in their briefcase. They have to win at all costs. Don't compete, just enjoy and find your own area of expertise somewhere else.

I discovered this early with a delicious Apple friend. We were playing a board game, and as usual, I was focused on everybody having a good time rather than who was winning. When my friend lunged across the table, almost knocking me off my chair so she could get to a piece first, I had the astonishing revelation that this was genuinely important to her. More than important—critical. I was shocked but learned a valuable lesson about Apples in a personal relationship.

If you try to clip an Apple's wings or dominate them, it won't be a long relationship. When the relationship does end and they're grieving, Apples push everything inside and cope with their misery silently. They put on a brave face for the world and surround themselves with the people who love them.

Ultimately, Apples can be amazing partners because they will never let the team falter financially. Their determination and resilience will give you strength though any crisis. You may well find yourself doing things you never thought you could.

Apple Stories in Four Different Flavours

This is the tale of Annette, whose **first and most extreme behavioural preference is Apple.** It's the story of what could happen depending on which Fruit she pairs with.

Annette and Basim: the Apple and the Banana

Apple Annette had long struggled to find a serious relation-ship. As senior partner in a celebrated law firm, she found men intimidated by her forthrightness, her status, and her need to be in control. She was naturally attracted to other high-flyer success types, but clashing travel schedules made it challenging for long term relationships, and when they were together, discussions seemed to degenerate into competition.

Then she met Basim, a Banana area manager for a large hardware chain. They met at a friend's party. They enjoyed each other's company and it was easy to spend the night together. Annette thought nothing of it; casual conquests weren't foreign to her. But Basim kept ringing for another date, and when she gave him one two months away, he took it. She assumed he'd lose interest and was mildly impressed when he sent flowers the week before the date, though she left them at the office because they were too much trouble to take home.

Basim pursued Annette and won her over. She loved his easy going manner and appreciated him working his travel schedule around hers. And it was pretty nice to come home to a cooked meal most nights of the week. On top of that, he was damned good at foot massages. When had a man ever given her a foot massage? Life settled and lust softened, but in fifteen years together they had their share of challenges.

In her personal life, Annette likes the same things she seeks in her business life: status, image, and power. She and Basim bought a home in the best neighbourhood, they send their children to the best school, and collect them in their luxury car. To the outside world, they seem to lead charmed lives. In reality, Annette works consistently to goals and she never, ever waivers in her belief that she will not fail.

Annette doesn't trust easily. Given her bloody-minded desire to succeed, she needs to stay in control of their finances. She manages their joint account and credit cards to keep ahead of the game. Basim is comfortable with that— more admin is something he does not need. He has his own account but doesn't really spend much on himself anyway. He's happy for Annette to take the lead.

When she asks Basim how his day was, he wants to tell her about all the issues at work, the politics, and the haggling. But he's learned over time that if he goes into the detail of his problems, he'd better be prepared to have them solved. He used to be so frustrated when Annette went into solving mode when all he wanted to do was to share.

These days, he's getting a business off the ground with two other partners, and from day one there's been conflict, which Basim can cope with but doesn't enjoy. When he's tried to talk it through with Annette she simply doesn't understand. Her only response is to fix the problem and she doesn't take anyone's feelings into account. Basim chooses what to share and when, often waiting until dinner when they can discuss their days, listen, and advise if necessary. He tells her when he wants her to help and asks that she listen when that's what he needs.

Basim is naturally adaptable and believes in giving second chances. He remembers that in the beginning, he loved the way Annette helped him with so many problems. He knows her ability to solve with such clarity is a gift. If he's willing to listen, Annette will always help him see another side of a problem he couldn't see before.

For years he went along with Annette's action-packed life. He wanted to please her and to be with her. They went skiing, even though he didn't like it much. They went trekking in Nepal, where the people were lovely, but the training was tedious. Annette excelled at everything she set her mind to and it was hard for Basim not to feel inadequate.

If you had asked her, Annette would have struggled to comprehend that Basim has his own needs. She would assume that they were the same as hers. She was so focused on her own goals and ambitions she was unaware of his. Banana Basim wasn't exactly trying to get his feelings noticed, so Annette assumed he loved doing the same things she did. Besides, she figured, doesn't her happiness equal Basim's happiness? Her pushiness to involve him in the same things she found stimulating and fulfilling was her way of showing she cared.

Eventually Basim made the decision to do the things that made him happy and choose carefully which activities he shared with Annette. That choice enabled him to create more balance in his life and be more content in his own skin. It never entered Annette's Apple mind to give up anything.

Basim smiles as he remembers the first time he took Annette for dinner with his closest friend. Bob had also invited another couple who Annette and Basim hadn't met. Annette had recently lost a lot of weight due to an illness she had kept very much to herself and close friends.

'How lovely to meet you,' said Madison as they were introduced. 'And look how thin and gorgeous you are! I'd love to be that thin. You must let me know your secret!'

'Here's the secret,' said Annette. 'Spend a month in hospital.'

During a long, drawn out, and very awkward silence, Annette held the gaze of unlucky Mango Madison. Mortified, Basim jumped in to introduce himself and move the topic skillfully away from Annette's illness. Unfortunately, it wasn't a good start to the night.

Annette had already labelled Madison as an imbecile. When she finally engaged in a decent conversation with Madison's husband Andrew, Basim shut it down because he thought it was getting too heated and religion wasn't something to discuss over dinner. Annette was more annoyed at that than Madison's ignorant comment. Why couldn't Basim step up to the plate?

Basim hovered around Annette, and tried to include her and share her achievements, and was overly devoted in refilling her wine glass or jumping up for more water. To cover his embarrassment and to compensate for Annette's stony silence, he talked too much. He felt physically ill that the evening had been ruined.

These days Basim is much more comfortable with himself and with who Annette is. She is not his responsibility nor is she a reflection on him. When these situations arise, he's ready to get on with being himself. He loves her but he is completely detached when she does or says something he doesn't agree with. They do, however, host more events than they attend. Annette enjoys it this way because she can control everything: the food, the wine, the venue, and the people.

In the early years, Basim found it tough to deal with what he saw as Annette's lack of emotion. Basim likes people; he's comfortable with them and has no problems expressing his feelings. He loves his fiery Apple and tells her so constantly. He knows he shows her love with all the things he does for her, from foot massages to special meals, to driving her to meetings when she's in a hurry. But when he didn't see the love coming back, he started to get resentful. He felt she was cold and distant. Nobody wants to have to remind someone to say, 'I love you.'

Annette saw Basim's loving nature and constant desire to do things together as being dependent on her. She saw herself as fiercely independent, needing no-one, and in encouraging Basim to do the same, she believed she was doing him a favour. Surely, by not hugging him or offering empathy when he wanted it.

When Basim finally raised this, Annette was genuinely surprised. She'd chosen to be with him, right? It was obvious she loved him and didn't need to say it to validate it. She considered a constant show of emotion, in public or in private, to be a lack of self-control. She had little time for illness and little compassion. If Basim was sick, she would leave him to it and go about her day as normal.

A few years into their relationship, Basim asked Annette to marry him. She said, 'No, there is no need.' Somewhat shocked, Basim took this as rejection. How could the woman he loved not want a beautiful wedding with all their friends around to celebrate? Didn't she love him?

He waited a while, then tried again and was told firmly this time there was no logical reason to get married. Annette told Basim if he could provide her with a logical reason, a business case, then she'd consider it. *Seriously?* Basim thought. *A business case?* He must be with a robot. Through Apple Annette's eyes, a wedding was a waste of time and money and would never change the way she felt about Basim. He felt she'd missed the whole point, and to this day is still hurt. Annette is not blessed with a natural empathy gene. As an extreme Apple, it's normal to be self-focused. She simply gets on with her life without stopping to think how anyone else may be feeling or how they might be affected by her actions. She expects Basim to speak up.

Basim is happy to do most of the domestic chores, though he wishes Annette was less selfish. When he raises it with her, she is stunned. Doesn't she provide the larger family income? Early on they agreed that she had the ability and the desire to make more money. Besides, she's very busy with her various activities. She believes that mastering all these new skills will benefit the family. Inside her head, it goes something like this: *By going to the gym each day, I'll be fitter and healthier and be able to play with my children and live longer. By taking a three month posting overseas away from the family, I'll come back a richer and more interesting person to be with. By going on trips with the girls twice a year, I'll be more relaxed, and be a nicer person at home. By studying for yet another degree, I'll be worth more in the marketplace and can bring in more dollars for the family. The same goes for the long working hours and extra projects. I'm making more money to make your life better!*

Basim has had to accept that Annette will do whatever she wants. This means he carries the load of domestic chores. He shops, cooks, washes, makes the kids' lunches, and ferries them to football practice. Annette likes to help with homework and that has become her domain.

Parenting has been a challenge for them. Annette is brutal when it comes to underachieving, and her children are no exception. At school, Annette was an A-grade student. It was simply not an option to do anything less than your absolute best. Needing her children to succeed was not only about them, it was about Annette's ego as well. She never fails. Having children who failed would make her a failure as a parent so she did everything in her power to ensure they got the very best marks possible, from providing the latest technology to helping them with research and managing their time.

Basim hated the pressure the kids were under. If they were upset from a day at school he'd rather sit on their bed and talk and hug, but Annette never lets up. There was no time for weakness. If they made a mistake, Basim was happy to write it off. Annette meters out punishments Basim feels are too harsh. When she sends a child to bed without dinner, Basim sneaks in a plate without her seeing. Annette raises her voice and denies requests. Basim goes into bat for the kids.

The school years were a traumatic time of arguments and frustration, often pushing Annette and Basim apart. If one thing tested their relationship more than anything else, it was their opposing styles of parenting. But the kids finished school with excellent grades and entered university. No-one was harmed in the making of this story.

The truth is that Apples care passionately for the core collection of people closest to them—family and maybe one or two friends who sneak in under the radar. Annette will fight to the death for her children and for the love of her life, Basim.

Over many years together, Basim has established what he likes to do and where his strengths lie and chosen his battles over the things that he feels need to change. Annette loves the nurturing home he's created for them and the comfort she feels with him to be herself. She loves that Basim is a confident individual with his own needs and interests. She recognises that he rarely asks for something to change, so when he does, she must take it seriously.

Annette and Basim lived happily ever after.

Apple and Banana

Bananas bring the warmth that Apples sometimes need. They give them a reason to come home and help develop their personal side. They have the empathy necessary to understand and care for their robust Apple. They love that their Apple is so focused and a strong decision-maker.

Apples need loyalty and a support team so Bananas provide the perfect foil, as long as Bananas can develop the strength to tackle their partners head on and are comfortable with their own independence.

Potential Problems

Apples can see Bananas natural tendency to give as a weakness. If they seem too needy, Apples will pull back as they need their partner to be self-sufficient. Apples are high achievers and it's easy for the Banana to feel inadequate. In a successful Apple-Banana relationship, it's crucial the Banana has a high level of self-esteem.

Apples are often unaware they have become controlling and dominating. Bananas can take too much personally when it is not intended that way.

Socially, Bananas get on with almost anyone. Apples have a low level of tolerance for those they see as incompetent, which can cause friction.

Annette and Marty: the Apple and the Mango

Apple Annette had long struggled to find a serious relationship. As a senior partner in a celebrated law firm, she found men intimidated by her forthrightness, her status, and her need to be in control. She was naturally attracted to other high-flyer success types, but clashing travel schedules made it challenging for long-term relationships, and when they were together, discussions always seemed to degenerate into a competition.

Then she met Marty, a Mango area manager for a large hardware chain, at a friend's party. They enjoyed each other's company and it was easy to spend the night together. Annette thought nothing of it; casual conquests weren't foreign to her. But Marty kept ringing for another date, and when she told him her first free night was two months away, he refused to believe it. He turned up at her office and convinced her to have coffee with him. A week later, he managed to take her for a drink. Finally, he got that dinner date.

It's a shame he didn't book that special restaurant ahead though. They couldn't get in. In fact, they couldn't get a table anywhere. Annette took control, opened an app on her phone, and found a restaurant. By the end of the meal, she was reluctantly charmed by Marty. She was convinced she could never be with someone so loose on detail, but his enthusiasm was infectious and he was a pretty damned exciting lover.

After a period of intense dating full of spontaneous weekends away, they became a thing. Annette loved Marty's zest for life. He was always up for adventure and he never said no. He came to every boring company function she had to attend and won over even the crustiest client. He kept up with the cracking pace she set and, together, life was a whirlwind.

But over the years they had their share of challenges. In her personal life, Annette likes the same things she seeks in her business life: status, image, and power. She and Marty bought a home in the best neighbourhood, they send their children to the best school, and collect them in their luxury car. Marty loves the status and indulges in a little showing off.

To the outside world, they seem to lead charmed lives. In reality, Annette works consistently to goals and she never, ever waivers in her belief that she will not fail.

It was therefore impossible that she could consider putting Marty in charge of the household budget. He is simply too … loose. He loves spending money and is very generous with their money. He's first to shout at the bar, even shout dinner, and is always looking for a new toy or planning a new holiday.

There have been many heated arguments about this, always ending in sex because that's Marty's answer to everything. Marty thinks Annette will forgive him for surely she can't be so intense? But Annette is unwavering in her need for control of the finances and therefore the future. In the end, they reach a compromise. Marty now keeps his own account for fun tickets and anything from their joint account must be discussed. Marty doesn't like having the brakes put on, but before long he's forgotten about it and moved on to the next shiny thing.

This became a problem. Marty was not exactly an efficiency machine and had a demanding job himself. If dinner wasn't organised, he didn't care. Go out! Order in! Oh, the breakfast dishes weren't put away. Never mind. And he's been too busy chatting with his daughter and sharing stories to make sure her homework is finished.

Annette has exploded so many times she's lost count. She resolves the problem by organising the week's meals and household chores and delegating some jobs to Marty while staying on his back to ensure he held his end up. As a Mango, Marty doesn't hang onto arguments and would rather be playing, so the issue was resolved.

Apple Annette and Mango Marty have now started a business together. Marty was keen to get into his own business to give him the freedom from authority, make his own decisions, and to create a fun workplace culture. The business idea was good, but Annette couldn't let him run it without her involvement. She found Marty's impulsiveness and inability to stop and think frustrating. She tried to debate strategy with him, but he was easily bored by politics and theories. Surprisingly, they made a great team. Both are big picture people. Marty has vision for the business and Annette's astute brain runs over each stage of the plan and ensures logistics and budgets will work. Both believe in employing others for detail and have built a small team with the skillsets they lack.

When there's a problem to be solved, both will reach a quick decision, although via different thought processes. Annette loves the challenge because she loves to fix things and Marty loves anything that keeps life exciting. He will jump to a solution using gut instinct, and Annette is there to back it up after thinking the problem through to a logical conclusion. Annette and Marty lead an action-packed life. In the beginning they did everything together, skiing, trekking, scuba diving.

Annette excelled at everything she set her mind to and was usually better than Marty, but he didn't mind at all. He was happy for her, and besides, she did the hard work to be the best. If he was bored, he moved on. He was happy to leave Annette to her own devices because his own life was jam packed. Just as well because it never entered Annette's mind to give up anything.

Marty nearly laughs out loud as he remembers the first time he took Annette for dinner with his closest friend. Bob had also invited another couple whom Annette and Marty hadn't met. Annette had recently lost a lot of weight due to an illness she had kept very much to herself and close friends.

'How lovely to meet you,' said Madison as they were introduced. 'And look how thin and gorgeous you are! I'd love to be that thin. You must let me know your secret!'

'Here's the secret,' said Annette. 'Spend a month in hospital.'

For a long, drawn out, awkward silence Annette held the gaze of the unlucky Mango Madison. Marty was the first to break the silence, bursting with laughter.

'That's my girl,' he says, wrapping an arm around her shoulder and squeezing tight. 'What I love about Annette is that you never have to second guess what she's thinking.'

Madison was apologetic but before long had jumped into another conversation, and while Annette thought she was an imbecile, she didn't let it ruin her night. Marty regaled the party with outrageous stories that had everyone in stitches, even Annette. She found herself drawn into an intense and stimulating conversation with Madison's husband Andrew, which more than made up for it.

Annette and Marty host more events than they attend. Annette enjoys it this way, because she can control everything: the food, the wine, the venue, and the people. As Marty loves food, wine, and people, together they stage brilliant dinner parties.

Marty struggled in the early years with what he saw as Annette's lack of emotion. Marty likes people; he's comfortable with them and has no problems expressing his feelings. He loves his fiery Apple and tells her all the time, showering her with gifts. When he didn't see the love coming back, Marty became resentful. He felt Annette was cold and distant. Nobody wants to have to remind someone to say, 'I love you.'

At first Annette enjoyed the gifts but after a while felt they were unnecessary, as was using up air space to say, 'I love you.'

When Marty raised the fact that Annette didn't love him back, she was genuinely surprised. She'd chosen to be with him, right? It was obvious she loved him and she didn't need to say it all the time to validate it. She saw the constant show of emotion, in public or in private, as a lack of self-control.

A few years into their relationship, Marty asked Annette to marry him. She said, 'No, there is no need.' Marty couldn't believe it. *How could the woman he loved not want a beautiful wedding, with all their friends around to celebrate? And most of all, how could she say no to him?* He waited a while before trying again and was told firmly this time there was no logical reason to get married. Annette challenged Marty to provide her with a logical reason, a business case, then she might consider it. *Seriously?* Marty thought, *who is this? Bloody Spock?* Apple Annette saw a wedding as a waste of time and money, which would never change the way she felt about Marty. Eventually he gave up and found other projects to distract himself with.

Annette is not blessed with a natural empathy gene. As an extreme Apple, she's self-focused. She simply gets on with her day without stopping to think how anyone else may be feeling or whether they'll be affected by what she's doing. Marty is okay with this most of the time, being self-absorbed, but even he's a little shocked by her lack of consideration for him and the family.

When he raises it with her, she is stunned. Doesn't she provide the larger family income? Early on, they agreed that she had the ability and the desire to make more money. Besides, she's busy with her various activities. She believes that mastering all these new skills will benefit the family. Inside her head it goes something like this: *By going to the gym each day, I'll be fitter and healthier and be able to play with my children and live longer. By taking a three-month posting overseas away from the family, I'll come back a richer and more interesting person to be with. By going on trips with the girls twice a year, I'll be more relaxed and be a nicer person at home. By studying for yet another degree, I'll be worth more in the marketplace and can bring more dollars into the family. The same goes for the long working hours and extra projects. I'm making more money to make your life better!*

Marty has had to reconcile himself to the fact that Annette will do whatever she wants. But that doesn't mean he's happy. He has to take on a lot more domestic chores and while he loves doing all the extra stuff with the kids, he's a bit sloppy on washing, and ironing is not an option. Annette likes to help with homework, so he lets her think that's her domain. In reality, he chooses the fun homework to help with, like drama and presentations, before she gets home.

Parenting has been a challenge for them. Annette is brutal when it comes to underachieving and her children are no exception. A-grades were a given. It was simply not an option not to put in your absolute best. Needing her children to succeed was not only about them, it was also about Annette's ego. Having children who failed would make her a failure as a parent. She did everything in her power to make sure that they got the very best marks possible, from providing the latest technology to helping them with research and managing their time.

By contrast, Marty would keep one of their daughters home from school if he hadn't seen her for a while. He would call the school with an excuse, then take her out for movies and ice cream. When Annette was away, he'd order in pizza. He'd let them stay up to see the full moon and race shopping trolleys down supermarket aisles.

Annette's approach to their children upset him. She never lets up. There was no time for weakness. If they made a mistake, Marty was happy to write it off, hoping it wouldn't happen again. Annette meters out punishments Marty feels are too harsh. If she sends a child to bed without dinner, Marty sneaks in bags of lollies and a packet of chips. Annette raises her voice and denies requests. Marty goes into bat for the kids and goes against Annette's wishes.

The school years were a traumatic time of arguments and frustration, often pushing Annette and Marty apart. He was frustrated with Annette's constant lecture mode and accused her of running their children as a business project. But the kids finished school with excellent grades and entry into university. And no-one was harmed in the making of this story.

The truth is that Apples care passionately for the core pocket of people closest to them: family and maybe one or two who may sneak in under the radar. Annette will fight to the death for her children and for the love of her life, Marty. She loves Marty's independence and that he has always made her laugh. Marty loves Annette's ability to make quick decisions and create new rules to suit her purpose.

Over many years together, Marty has acquiesced to many of Annette's wishes but quietly gone rogue on several things, from secret parenting and secret spending to secret affairs. Marty's ego never recovered from the fact that Annette wouldn't marry him. The cracks started way back before they had children and never really healed. He needed way more attention than Annette was willing to provide and started having not so discreet liaisons. Eventually he met someone who could love him back the way he wanted. Annette and Marty went their separate ways.

Apple and Mango

Life moves quickly, conflict is resolved, and nobody gets too hurt. Apples should look after the budget and Mangoes plan the holidays. They are both independent and meld in their desire to have the freedom to do what they want. They enjoy shooting the breeze in a conceptual way without drilling down to detail. Mangoes admire Apple's quick decision-making. Apples enjoy Mango's sense of adventure and their ability to see fun in everything which can bring out the playfulness in Apple.

Potential Problems

Apples are frustrated by Mango's inability to stop and think. They start to see the Mango as lacking control and too impulsive about everything, from food to emotions. Mangoes can disappoint Apples because they're not much of a debating partner. They're easily bored and don't really enjoy conflict. Mangoes get sick of the Apple's control and regular lecture mode and become bored with the constant business conversation.

Annette and Lucy: the Apple and the Lime

Apple Annette had always struggled to find a serious relationship. As a senior partner in a celebrated law firm, she found others were intimidated by her forthrightness, status, and need to be in control. She was naturally attracted to other high-flyer success types, but clashing travel schedules made it challenging for long-term relationships. When they were together, discussions seemed to degenerate into a competition.

Then she met Lucy, a Lime area manager for a large hardware chain, at a friend's party. They enjoyed each other's company and it was easy to spend the night together. Annette thought nothing of it; casual conquests weren't foreign to her. She was surprised when Lucy followed up a week later with a carefully thought out text.

Annette decided to give it a shot and booked a date two months away. She assumed Lucy would lose interest in that time, but was mildly impressed when, two weeks out, Lucy sent a detailed email offering a choice of two restaurants, with reservations in place. Annette liked Lucy immediately. She didn't push. She loved her contained manner and ability to bring a sense of calm and order to Annette's high-powered life and long hours. Coming home at night meant entering a world of order and predictability. Life settled and lust softened. But in fifteen years together they had their share of challenges.

In her personal life, Annette seeks the same things as her business life: status, image, and power. She and Lucy bought a home in the best neighbourhood, they send their children to the best school, and collect them in their luxury car. To the outside world, they seem to lead charmed lives. In reality, Annette works consistently to goals and she never, ever waivers in her belief that she will not fail.

Annette doesn't trust easily. Given her relentless desire to succeed, she has always been in control of finances in any relationship she has had. But it was different with Lucy. With an innate skill for detail and spotting problems, Annette had to grudgingly admit that household finances were best left to Lucy—and it has freed her up to focus on the big picture like deciding on where to go on holidays. Lucy would pick up the thread and run with it, booking flights, accommodation, and tours. They have joint bank accounts as both are careful with money and respectful of each other's hard-earned cash.

With Lucy, life happens the way Annette wants it. Of course, there are times when Lucy loses it, but the house almost always operates with military precision.

Lucy doesn't hassle Annette about her day the minute she walks in the door. She gives her space to help with homework, eat dinner with the family, and finally, when the kids are off playing, Lucy and Annette sit down to talk about their day over a glass of wine.

Annette prefers to give a top line summary, editing out needless detail. Lucy, on the other hand, is like a cascading waterfall of information. In an effort to stem the flow and move the conversation along, Annette continually cuts Lucy off, trying to solve her problems. This results in frustration on both sides; Lucy because she feels Annette doesn't listen, Annette because Lucy can't see the solution clearly. Annette can't understand why Lucy is so needy. She doesn't need anyone's help to solve her own problems. Most of the time, Lucy just shuts down and that finishes the conversation.

These days, Lucy is getting a business off the ground with two other partners, and from day one there's been conflict, which she has struggled to cope with. When she's tried to talk it through with Annette, her answer is just to fix it. She doesn't seem to take anyone's feelings into account. After a while, Lucy stops sharing her business problems with Annette unless it's around strategy.

For years, Lucy was barely aware that Annette was driving their lives, despite an underlying reluctance to do everything Annette planned. They went skiing, even though Lucy hated to ski. They went trekking with a group in Nepal, and Lucy was exhausted just being around so many people all the time. And Annette excelled at everything she set her mind to. It was hard for Lucy not to feel inadequate. If you asked Annette, she would've struggled to comprehend that Lucy had her own needs. She was so focused on her own goals and ambitions she was unaware of Lucy's.

Lime Lucy wasn't exactly trying to get her feelings noticed, so Annette just assumed Lucy's needs were the same as hers, and they loved doing the same things. Besides, doesn't her happiness equal Lucy's happiness? Annette's pushiness to involve them both in the activities she found stimulating and fulfilling was her way of showing she cared. As time went by, Lucy began to pull back from all the action-packed accomplishments Annette pushed herself through. She couldn't compete so she began to develop her own interests, things she enjoyed on her own.

Lucy still cringes as she remembers the first time she took Annette to have dinner with her closest friend. Bob had also invited another couple who Annette and Lucy hadn't met. Annette had recently lost a lot of weight due to an illness she had kept very much to herself and close friends.

'How lovely to meet you,' said Madison as they were introduced. 'And look how thin and gorgeous you are! I'd love to be that thin. You must let me know your secret!'

'Here's the secret,' said Annette. 'Spend a month in hospital.'

During a long, drawn out, awkward silence, Annette held the gaze of the unlucky Mango Madison. The silence continued as Lucy slowly died inside for everyone: Bob, herself, Annette, Madison, and Madison's husband Andrew. Bob finally broke the silence to usher everyone to drinks.

It wasn't a good start to the night. Annette had already labelled Mango Madison as an imbecile. Lucy recoiled into herself and was quieter than normal. She sat silently all night, replaying the embarrassing moment in her head. Her stomach was tied in knots with Annette's behaviour. She was appalled. Annette recovered and engaged in a robust conversation with Madison's husband Andrew. Lucy was inwardly seething. How could she be so relaxed after being so rude?

These days she accepts Annette for who she is. After being together for so long, Lucy knows that Annette is likely to drop these bombshells every now and then. But equally, she has learned that the way Annette acts and reacts is no reflection on Lucy as her partner.

They do, however, host more events than they attend—both prefer it this way. Lucy takes joy in the planning, and Annette can control everything: the food, the wine, the venue, and the people.

Other people often comment on what they see as Annette's lack of emotion. But Lucy knows better. Annette is fiercely protective of her, provides her with a safe, stable home, and in private, shows plenty of affection. Lucy doesn't demand attention, she does not enjoy excessive and public displays of affection. She would like her partner to say, 'I love you,' more often, but understands that Annette shows her love in other ways.

A few years into their relationship, Lucy raised the topic of marriage. She was quietly keen but with Annette not being much of a romantic, she didn't think she would go for it. And she didn't. Annette was firmly against marriage. She considers it an old fashioned and unnecessary institution. For Apple Annette, a wedding was a waste of time and money, and would never change the way she felt about Lucy. Lucy would have liked a wedding, mainly for her parents and family, but she couldn't deny the pragmatism of Annette's approach.

Annette is not blessed with a natural empathy gene. As an extreme Apple, she's naturally self-absorbed. She gets on with her day without stopping to think how anyone else may be feeling or how they'll be affected by what she's doing. If Lucy has an issue, Annette expects her to speak up.

This is one of their biggest areas of discontent. In the face of Apple strength, Lucy is often reluctant to voice her opinion. She chooses instead to fume quietly and withdraw until Annette eventually notices and an argument ensues. Annette is frustrated that Lucy has been ruminating in silence, and Lucy's anger has boiled under the surface for so long she explodes.

Lucy is content to do most of the domestic chores, though she wishes Annette was less selfish. When she raises it with her, Annette is stunned. Doesn't she provide the larger family income? Early on, they agreed that she had the ability and the desire to make more money. Besides, she's busy with her various activities. She believes that her mastering all these new skills will benefit the family. Inside her head it goes something like this: *By going to the gym each day, I'll be fitter and healthier and be able to play with my children and live longer. By taking a three-month posting overseas away from the family, I'll come back a richer and more interesting person to be with. By going on trips with the girls twice a year, I'll be more relaxed, making me a nicer person at home. By studying for yet another degree, I make myself worth more in the marketplace, so I can bring more dollars into the family. The same goes for the long working hours and extra projects. I'm making more money to make your life better!*

Lucy has to accept that Annette will do whatever she wants. This means she ends up with most of the domestic chores. She shops, cooks, washes, packs the kids' lunches, and takes them to football practice. As it turns out, she's happy with her role as she knows all will be done properly, to her own high standard.

Annette likes to help with homework so that has become her domain. She is brutal when it comes to underachieving and her children are no exception. A-grades are a given. It's simply not an option not to work, stress, or put in your very best. Needing her children to succeed was not all about them; it was about Annette's ego as well. Having children who failed would make her a failure as a parent. She did everything in her power to ensure that they achieved the best possible marks, from providing the latest technology to helping them with research and managing their time.

Lucy was quietly supportive. She may not have been quite as hard as Annette, but she believed in driving for perfection and in this way, she and Annette were in sync. On parenting matters, they were often on the same page, presenting a united front. Tears were for private moments, resilience was called for, and mistakes were never, ever to be repeated.

Apples care passionately for the core pocket of people closest to them – family and one or two who sneak in under the radar. Annette will fight to the death for her children, and for the love of her life, Lucy. Over many years together, Annette and Lucy have reached a comfortable and respectful relationship. Lucy has learned to pick her battles, to speak up and stick to her guns when something matters to her. She knows the best times to tackles issues and has the facts backing her up.

Annette loves the stability and security Lucy brings to their home. She can save her energy and arguments for the courtroom as they rarely argue at home. Together they run a tight ship. They're a solid team, representing financial and emotional security. They have a deep love for each other, respect each other's differences and at this stage are living happily together.

Apple and Lime

Apples and Limes gel on their pragmatic side and Limes offer the reliability and stability that Apples seek. Both share strong family values and together can build a solid foundation. Limes think highly of Apple's work ethic and seriousness, admiring their quick, logical decision-making, their drive, and ambition. Apples love Lime's loyalty and steadiness. They know they can safely leave the financial details of daily life to their Lime partner, allowing them to get on with bigger projects.

Potential Problems

Apple's workaholic nature and inability to notice the minutiae of family life can be hugely frustrating for Limes who live by rules and structure. When an Apple is late home, misses a school concert, or leaves a dinner party to take calls, Limes can get nitpicky and nagging. Apples interpret nagging as a means of control, so they raise their voice and refuse to co-operate.

Although both enjoy domestic quiet time, Limes will comfortably settle down and nest, but Apples still need activities and challenges outside the home. Unless the Lime can deal with this independence, the relationship could well go pear-shaped.

Annette and Archie: a Pair of Apples

Apple Annette had long struggled to find a serious rela-tionship. As a partner in a celebrated law firm, she found others were intimidated by her forthrightness, status, and need to be in control. She was naturally attracted to other high-flyer success types, but clashing travel schedules made it challenging for long-term relationships, and when they were together, discussions seemed to degenerate into competition.

One evening at a friend's party, she met Archie, another Apple and area manager for a large hardware chain. They enjoyed each other's company and it was easy to spend the night together. Annette thought nothing of it; casual conquests weren't foreign to her. She was surprised when she found herself wanting to see Archie again, and when he called a couple of days later, they found a date they were both available within a few weeks. They discussed where they would go and agreed on a restaurant which Archie booked.

Annette liked Archie a lot. His conversation was sti-mulating, and he didn't shy away from a good argument. He kept up with her cracking pace. She didn't feel impatient or agitated as she did around so many others, waiting for them to catch up with her thoughts. She had met her match and she liked it very much. Life was full on and driven; they moved forward with purpose together. But in fifteen years, they had their share of challenges.

A double Apple means a tsunami of emotional intensity that takes maturity and real love to navigate through. Each person wants control. Each is low on the empathy gene. And both need to be right.

Annette seeks the same things in her personal life as she does professionally: status, image, and power. She and Archie bought a home in the best neighbourhood, they send their children to the best school, and collect them in their luxury car. To the outside world, they seem to lead charmed lives. In reality, both work consistently to achieve their goals and they never, ever waiver in their belief that they will not fail.

Annette doesn't trust easily. Given her relentless desire to succeed, she has always been in control of finances in any relationship she has had. Archie was the same. He didn't trust easily, he was driven to succeed, and as close as Annette came to being someone he could trust, he needed to look after the finances. For years they kept separate accounts, splitting bills and holiday costs. But when the children came along, Archie began looking after the household finances.

Archie and Annette are on the same page so it would seem there is no problem—except both are expecting that someone else will manage the housework. When it was just the two of them, Annette and Archie ate out most nights. They both work long hours and enjoy spending time together over dinner on the way home. On weekends, they share the cleaning. After they had children, they hired a live-in nanny, a cleaner, and a gardener. They also had Annette's parents, who lived nearby and were always happy to lend a hand, and

Annette and Archie were happy to take their help. Each of them juggled busy professional lives and numerous conflicting activities. Over time, dinner together became rare.

The reality of two Apples together, particularly if there are children involved, is that one Apple, the less dominant one, will end up defaulting to their second and sometimes third personality preferences. With two fiery types, both wanting control and needing things their way, there is little time or desire left for the practical and mundane matters of running house and family. When both are in superpower mode, the energy that fills their home is a force to be reckoned with.

But when children came along, Annette and Archie's lifestyle was not sustainable. Something had to give. Somebody had to be the support act and Annette was surprised to discover she was the one who pulled back. Archie wanted a CEO role and the demands on the family were simply too high. Her career plans to become a barrister and later a judge would have to go on hold. As failure or not achieving her goals is not an option for Annette, she took the appropriate Apple action and reframed her goals.

These days, Annette has taken her passion for commercial law and started her own firm with two other partners. This gives her the flexibility she needs for family and fulfils her need to be in control of her own career. She can manage the children and their pathways through school and continue to have mentally stimulating conversations with Archie.

Apple-Apple is a dynamic combination. Annette and Archie took holidays that tested their skills and their relationship. They skied the black runs, and their Nepalese trek became a race to beat other travellers to the next village. There was never a feeling of inadequacy, just an intense desire to get the best result at everything they did.

As life went on and career demanded more of their time, Annette and Archie explored separate interests. They would occasionally run a marathon together, but each was prone to setting their own goal to achieve—from climbing a higher mountain peak to winning the local art prize.

Archie smiles as he remembers the first time he took Annette to have dinner with his closest friend. Bob had also invited another couple whom Annette and Archie hadn't met. Annette had recently lost a lot of weight due to an illness she had kept very much to herself and close friends.

'How lovely to meet you,' said Madison as they were introduced. 'And look how thin and gorgeous you are! I'd love to be that thin. You must let me know your secret!'

'Here's the secret,' said Annette. 'Spend a month in hospital.'

During a long, drawn out, awkward silence, Annette held the gaze of the unlucky Mango Madison. Archie let the silence continue as he secretly enjoyed the pain on the faces of everyone around, except his wonderful, straightforward, honest, Annette. Bob finally broke the silence to usher everyone to drinks. As Annette had already labelled Madison as an imbecile, she turned to her husband Andrew to see if he stood up to the test and ended up enjoying a robust conversation with him and Archie.

Social issues are not often a problem for Annette and Archie. If they don't like people, they don't accept the invitation. If they're not having a good time, they leave. If some people see their directness as offensive, so be it. After being together for many years, they know they are both capable of dropping clangers every now and then, and truth be known, they quite enjoy it. They do, however, host more events than they attend, where they can control everything: the food, the wine, the venue, and the guests.

Archie's friends often comment on what they see as Annette's lack of emotion. They want someone "softer" for Archie, but Archie knows better. Annette is fiercely protective of him, contributes to an emotionally and financially stable life, and shows him affection in the privacy of their home. Neither one is big on saying, "I love you". It didn't become an issue as both knew their love for each other was solid. A few years into their relationship, Archie raised the topic of marriage. At first, Annette was firmly against it, considering marriage an old-fashioned institution that wasn't required to show their love.

But together they looked at the logistics of bringing up children, and it gave them a good excuse for an extravagant holiday. They liked the idea of consolidating goals and the idea of marriage made them feel more powerful together. They planned a small wedding in front of close friends and family and tied a strong knot. They were a formidable team.

As their family grew and it became obvious that one of them would have to pull back, they addressed matters from a practical perspective. Archie provided the larger family income and had soaring ambitions to be CEO of a large firm. But Annette demanded compromise. If she was to spend more time at home with their family, she wanted the opportunity for time away. Three times a year she would travel with the girls or take a study break. Archie agreed to Annette's proposal and, in principle, it should have worked—but when Annette was ready to take time off, it was never convenient for Archie. They had some next level Apple arguments but Annette refused to back down. In the end, Archie backed down a little, but mainly they called on their parents to help look after the children.

Annette is brutal when it comes to underachieving and her children are no exception. A-grades were a given. It was simply not an option to put in less than your absolute best. Needing her children to succeed was about Annette's ego as well. Having children who failed would make her a failure as a parent. She did everything in her power to ensure they got the best marks possible, providing the latest technology and helping them with research and managing their time. Archie supports Annette's drive for their children to succeed, but he's not around much to take the load, and he simply doesn't care as much as Annette does. He knows she will drive them to achieve their maximum potential to become children he can be proud of. On parenting, they were usually on the same page, presenting a united front. Tears were for private moments, resilience was called for, and mistakes were never, ever to be repeated.

Apples care passionately for the core group of people closest to them—family and one or two who sneak in under the radar. Annette will fight to the death for her children and for the love of her life, Archie.

Over many years together, Annette and Archie have settled into their roles. Their marriage is regulated by a deep and binding respect for each other and an appreciation of each other's strengths. They spend time planning and goal setting, for their children, in their careers, and for pleasure. They enjoy the fast pace and logic of each other's minds. They value intellect, have a stimulating mental and physical relationship, and have no need to constantly explain themselves. They are obsessive in their love for each other, fiercely protective but also fiercely independent. Annette and Archie are a formidable team. If you choose to cross them, you had better be prepared.

Double Apple

The Apple double act is never dull. Both value independence, both think quickly, and enjoy intense, intellectual discussion. Highly competitive, they may take on a new activity together, but rarely stick to it. They prefer to do their own thing, for fear their internal competition may implode the relationship. Apple minds are often filled with new challenges which makes them seem preoccupied, but with two Apples, neither is offended or feels the need to fill gaps.

Potential Problems

The biggest danger is to focus too much on their own journeys and forget to love each other. Meals together can become rare as both juggle careers and conflicting activities. Their children will benefit from astute advice, but the parents must take care not to lose each other along the way.

How to handle the Apple in your life

Love yourself. In a relationship with an Apple, it's particularly important that you maintain and develop strong self-esteem. Don't expect compliments. Your Apple is glowing with pride on the inside, but doesn't feel the need to say it. When you're not hearing, "I love you" or feeling enough love, remind them that they need to be more involved. But remember, this doesn't come easily for them and we all expect love in the same form that we give it. Your Apple loves you but doesn't want to get all public and mushy about it.

Develop your own hobbies and interests so when your partner is away for months at a time, or working all night, you can operate independently. Choose something you love to do and improve at your own pace. Your Apple partner will gain great respect for your independence and for not relying on them to provide your happiness or fulfilment.

If you're a little fragile, don't try to compete with them. Take up skydiving if you enjoy it but know that your Apple will always need to be better than you. Like a racehorse, they run faster when anyone edges up on them. They love to be one step ahead.

Choose your battles. Arguing with an Apple can get ugly, so diffuse unnecessary fights with neutral tone and calm comments. Don't go after the big win—aim for compromise or trade-offs—where your Apple partner can maintain dignity. Let them retire from an argument they've clearly lost by smiling and saying little. They know they might just be wrong and they know you know it. But let them know you're onto them.

If they do lose their temper and it feels out of control, back off. Let it cool and resume the discussion at another time. Remember, Apples will often sound more aggressive than they are. Go head to head but don't lose your cool, but stand firm. Match their pace and tone. Appeal to reason, and to feelings. If you're gunning for Christmas with your family, don't tell them Mum and Dad will be hurt if you don't go. Tell them the airfares and accommodation you save by not going to their family can be spent on the new TV.

If you constantly make your feelings known in the relationship, it will help avoid conflict later. Even if they don't remember, you can keep a tally and whip it out. Your Apple partner will be counting on you to be the glue in the relationship. If you're not holding it all together, they'll come unstuck. Don't throw away all the good bits by trying to measure who loves who more.

Remember, they need to be number one; to be the breadwinner, to earn more, to be more successful. For you to be successful in love with your Apple, accept, admire, and respect this part of them.

Tips for Apples

We all know you're good at solving problems. The danger is how you deliver the solution, and solving it the way you want all the time. Beware of sounding parental. Your partner will start feeling like a child. Remember that your partner may want support, not solutions. Try asking questions before bowling in with advice.

Give your partner and your children a chance to make their own mistakes, even though every bone in your body is screaming, "Stop!" When you stop them, you are preventing them creating a roadmap and guidelines for their own journey.

Practice leaving your bossy work pants in the car when you get home and be aware that your tendency to control may cause resentment. In conflict, understand that you can appear more intimidating or aggressive than you think. Smiling helps and so can lowering volume or changing tone. Be prepared for your partner to take your feedback personally and try not to overreact.

If you are doggedly focused on the activities that please you, and only you, then you are going to lose time with your partner. Too much time apart means you drift in different directions. If you have children, this can mean your partner is at home taking care of them and their own needs go unmet. This can make them feel inferior and create an unhealthy relationship—one where you have all the control. Every time you choose to do something just for you, something that will take you away from family time, ask yourself, 'Is this just for me or will it really move the family forward?'

Make a list of non-work leisure activities such as picnics or going out to lunch and include some non-competitive activities such as yoga. Maybe consider trying one?

Practice asking your partner a question about them once a day. The question: *What do you think about me?* does not count. Think about what makes them happy. Do they love a tidy backyard? Flowers? A new bar to visit on a Friday night? Aim to give them an experience or gift they value. Once a week, at the very least, ask your partner if there's something you can do for them. Practice giving compliments out loud, not just thinking them. Try saying *I love you* without an action attached. For example: 'Can you pick up some milk on the way home? Love you!' is not the way to say *I love you*.

Observe how you react to criticism. Do you naturally go on the attack? Try listening first without judging. If you're prone to anger quickly, make a list of what triggers this response. Many Apples report it's due to issues of control, that is the other person is not doing what they want in the way that they want it. If this is the case, choose your battles. You don't have to win ALL the time.

Once you've had your say, let it go. Don't constantly return to it. Remember, it's okay to be wrong or to compromise every now and again! It's also good to say you're sorry when you are. These simple words can have a powerful impact. Crying is not a weakness; it is a way of expressing emotion, along with anger, raising your voice, slamming a door, or going silent. Adjust your lens to see it as such.

It's not always your job to tell the truth the way you see it. Sometimes it's hurtful and unnecessary, especially if the other person is aware of their mistake. Stop and think before you release a blast: is this for you or for them?

Short and Sweet

Apples in a relationship

- obsessive about their partner
- only do what they like around the house
- spend long hours at work
- love vibrant, heated debates
- dislike conflict at a personal level
- need to be in control
- prone to solving first
- will justify everything they do as for the good of the family.

Apple sticking points

- hate to be wrong, quick to blame
- self-absorbed with goals
- unsociable when they're bored
- private and public displays of affection don't come easily
- don't like to discuss their emotions
- always think they're right
- need to do things better than you.

Mixed Fruit

Apple-Banana: Bananas bring warmth, empathy, patience, and Apples love their loyalty and ability to love. Apples get frustrated with a Banana's lack of independence. Bananas get frustrated with Apple's lack of tolerance in social situations.

Apple-Mango: both like results and move quickly. Apples like Mango's sense of adventure and playfulness. Mangoes like Apple's action, rule-breaking, and decisions. Apples get frustrated with Mango's lack of control and logic, Mangoes with Apple's constant lectures and control.

Apple-Lime: both are pragmatic. Apples like Lime's loyalty and sense of safety. Limes like Apple's work ethic, drive, and seriousness. Apples tire quickly of Lime's nagging and nit-picking: Limes get frustrated with Apple's inability to deal with domestic detail.

Double Apples: have mutual respect for intellect and inde-pendence. Apples compete and can become so self-focused they forget to make time for each other.

Handling an Apple

- love yourself
- develop your own interests
- don't expect compliments
- accept that you are better at giving unconditional love
- choose your battles
- accept, respect, and admire the fact that your delicious Apple needs to be number one
- don't tie your own self-esteem to their hugs and I love yous
- be direct when you confront them.

Tips for Apples

- support, don't always solve
- let others make their own mistakes
- choose your external activities to fit with family
- try asking your partner what they want
- try a non-competitive sport
- watch how and when your anger sparks ask yourself if it's always about control
- give compliments.

Chapter 8

Mesmerised by Mangoes

Living with a Mango may be messy, unpredictable, and dis-organised, but it will never be boring. They live their lives in glorious colour and see nothing but possibilities in it. **Mangoes only have two speeds: fast and asleep.** They clean their teeth in the shower, go the long way round to avoid traffic lights, and leave their clothes on the floor for an easy pick up the next day. Like a pinball machine, they're constantly zinging around the house, tapping a foot, clicking a pen, drumming to the sound in their head.

Nothing goes fast enough for a Mango. They skim the business headlines and go straight for the human-interest stories like sport and murder. They'll skip all over the news but get bored before one article is finished.

Mangoes are always last to bed just in case they miss something. They can be exhausted, but no way will they cancel a party. It may be the last night of their lives, and what if something exciting happens? They drag their tired bodies out of the house and as they enter the party, something magical happens: the switch is pulled, the lights are on, and it's showtime!

Mangoes don't want to relax on the weekends with books and bingeing on TV series. I mean, that's okay for a limited time, but not all day. What else are we doing? They need to know that their time is productive and they're not wasting a minute of their life. You may find them in front of the television, but they'll be checking social media, chatting on WhatsApp, and have a cake in the oven at the same time.

Mangoes love to be loved and measure their popularity by the number of friends they have. The concept of "friends" has taken on a whole new meaning with the arrival of social media, where friends and followers are a benchmark of Mango popularity. You'll notice that those who post most excluding influencers will all have a Mango bent. Look at your social media friends.

Mangoes are happiest in an electric, excited atmosphere where the focus is on them. An actor friend of mine says there's nothing quite like the end of a play, when you're bathing in the glory of applause and adulation. His challenge is to find that happiness in everyday life.

Because they love to be the centre of attention, Mangoes often focus the conversation on themselves. This isn't calculated. They simply believe their stories are more interesting. They also feel that if there's a lull in conversation, it's their duty to fill it with something fabulous about themselves. And their stories are always dialled up. Always. Watch your Mango friend on social media or listen to them on the phone. They are simply going about their lives, like you and I. But they don't go grocery shopping. They scream into the supermarket, only just manage to get a park, grab whatever was closest from the shelves (who knows what we'll end up eating for dinner?) and only just miss out on a parking ticket because they parked illegally. Their lives are always designed to look more exciting than yours, although not always intentionally.

At this extreme end, Mangoes have little respect for the sensitivity of others, as they're not sensitive folk themselves. **They tend to see everything as funny** and can't understand why others don't. In their minds, everything is translated into pictures, often cartoons, explaining why they can laugh at inappropriate times. Mangoes aren't immune to feeling hurt, but being the actors they are, they're good at covering it up. They're the ones who smile and laugh a bit too loudly when they're eliminated on a reality TV show. At home, they may act as if everything is fine, but later withdraw into themselves, leaving their partner wondering what's wrong.

It's easy to fall in love with a Mango personality, and many people are drawn into their irresistible orbit. We're attracted by their self-confidence, natural charisma, and their optimism, but possibly the very best thing is they bring unselfconscious, joyous fun to a partnership.

For their part, Mangoes are drawn to people on impulse and follow a relationship for no other reason than it feels right. They genuinely enjoy spending time with people, are skilled at reading them, and like making them happy. Extreme Mangoes, however, find it hard to be monogamous in their constant quest for new experiences. They love the spontaneity and discovery of a new relationship, but when they tire of it, they often find themselves in a situation where the other person is in love. For the Mango, it was all just a bit of fun and they don't know how to extract themselves.

A friend of mine told me of someone who'd been chasing her for some time. He sent erotic texts and phone calls, all of which she enjoyed, but which she never took further—because all the world knew that not only was Mango Max married, he also played the same game with a number of women.

But for both sexes, the pull of Mango charm is magnetic. Many times my partner and I have walked away from our first meeting with a Mango with whom we've enjoyed a stimulating and buoyant conversation, only to acknowledge we both had fallen for him.

Mangoes like to look good, but don't obsess with detail. They love the drop-in. Another audience! Not the best of housekeepers, they don't worry about the state of the house and are very happy to make do with the lick and a promise approach to housework. Tidying up means shoving everything in the wardrobe and slamming the door shut. Housework is done randomly, preferably to music you can dance to.

Mainly, they'll just clean up if they're having visitors, but even that's random because they get bored so quickly. Because they get so easily distracted, they can start putting clean sheets on the bed and leave it halfway because they think of cleaning the oven and then leave it halfway because they remember to take the garbage downstairs and then ... you will know what I'm talking about if you've ever lived with a Mango.

Because Mangoes have several things on the go at once, they don't stop to find a sock that's missing in the wash. Instead, they throw them all in a drawer, which means they often end up wearing odd socks because in their rush to get dressed, they can't find a matching pair. Or they buy more.

Many Mangoes have confided in me that because they forget to do the washing regularly, they often drag something out from the bottom of the dirty clothes basket, dust it off, and brazenly wear it to a meeting. More still tell me that when they run out of clean undies, they don't wear any.

There's no embarrassment for wardrobe malfunctions of any sort, a thread hanging here, a tear there, a missing button. All that belongs in the detail folder and Mangoes are impatient with detail, planning, finances, and routine. Let's take the example of choosing a healthcare fund. Somehow, this job fell to Mango me.

I prepared myself to work through this administrative minefield. I spoke to several providers but didn't really understand any of them. I went to my Lime brother-in-law for help, knowing he would have done all this research and be able to tell me straight away which fund to choose. But he didn't solve my problem! He thought he was being helpful by directing me to a website which compared health funds. "You can't go wrong," were his words. But there was too much to read, it took too much time and so … I stayed with the same fund, where I'm certainly paying far too much.

Living with Mango unpunctuality and disregard for rules can be a challenge for their often Lime partners. Because of a Mango's inability and reluctance to handle the mundane, it's hard for Limes to find routine and structure. Mangoes put too much on their "to do" list each day in their desire to do everything they possibly can. Then they run out of time, and then, they're late.

While Lime sits in the car clenching his jaw, Mango will be hunting for lost keys, wallet, mobile, or that important document that was "here a minute ago". Partners can help by knowing this will happen; have their stuff ready, create a special Lost and Found Mango place in the house.

For strong Mangoes, it's as natural as breathing to test the limits in every area of their lives. Financially, this can become a sticking point. Mangoes make money to spend. They never set any aside for a rainy day—you could be dead tomorrow. If there's a new cliff to jump off, they must try it. They never worry about running out of money because they know they will always find a way around it, so they spend, and enjoy the moment. Some would call it frivolous.

Mangoes live in the moment. This impulsive trait means everything they do or have is for now. They don't save the crystal glasses for guests and they don't have a formal sitting room. They're first to get the latest model phone, see the new release film, or visit the restaurant that opened this week. Self-control doesn't rate much in their world.

If you have a Mango partner, enjoy their energy and zest for life because they'll give you experiences that you may never have had. Life may be a tsunami when you choose a Mango partner, but it will never, ever be dull.

A Mango story in four different flavours.

This is the tale of Mitch, **whose first behavioural preference is extreme Mango**. It's the story of what might happen depending on which Fruit he pairs with.

Mitch and Lauren: the Mango and the Lime

Handsome Mitch swept Lauren off her feet. Working for a global telco, he travels most weeks but calls her regularly. She is the centre of his universe. He buys her extravagant gifts, sends flowers for no reason, and delights her with secrets and surprises. Her friends tell her she has struck gold. Mitch is all style and Lauren feels good going out with him by her side. He is irresistible company and charms her friends with his entertaining stories. Lauren soon discovers that Mango and drama go hand in hand. Mitch has a flair for theatrics.

Mitch: You wouldn't believe it! This guy was after me and he was the size of three houses, full of muscle, and honestly more than 6 feet (190 centimetres) tall! I had no hope of escape ... I was boxed in and I could feel the sweat streaming down my back, down my legs, until my socks were damp. His eyes locked on mine and I could hear him growl as he snarled and almost took a lunge at me. Thank goodness for the security guards, who got to me just as he was close enough for me to smell the beer on his breath.

Mitch's world plays out in vibrant colour with characters painted big and bold. He doesn't live life on the sideline. He is always in the game where even the mundane becomes good theatre.

At first puzzled and then frustrated, Lauren wants to interrupt Mitch with questions and detail. How tall was he? Where did this happen? How come there were security guards at the game? But you weren't wearing socks that day! Lauren has learnt to smile. It's pure entertainment. She can get specifics when it matters. She knows not to ruin his stories, even if she's heard them before. She loves that socialising is so effortless for Mitch. It takes the pressure off her. Life is a whirlwind as Mitch creates a pool of activities and friends to choose from.

When they married, Mitch was the perfect groom. Nothing was too much trouble to create Lauren's dream wedding. She wanted a special venue. Mitch found a Scottish castle. She wanted unusual transport; he gave her six white horses and an 18th century carriage. Without Mitch, she would never have planned such an extravagant wedding.

Like any extreme Mango, Mitch is a combination of actor and chameleon. With his desire to avoid sameness, he loves trying different things, so when they first met, it was only natural Lauren thought she'd won the lottery. Mitch seemed to like all the things she did. He went to art galleries with her, started long-distance running with her, and helped write lyrics to her music. His sense of freedom and lack of inhibition was intoxicating. Then, like any couple who've been together for a while, the initial excitement and romance dimmed a little and Lauren began to face the reality of life with Mitch the Mango.

He talked all the time. And every story she told he'd have to top with a better story. When they were out, he talked over her, even answered for her. 'Oh sure, Lauren would love that,' even when she was standing right there. It started to get under her skin, and she began to disappear into her shell while he took over.

Lauren had misinterpreted Mitch's chameleon-like flexibility and sense of adventure: she thought he liked all the things she did. He was sincere in his desire to make her happy and committed to trying new things but once art galleries and writing lyrics were no longer new, he was soon bored. This was a natural progression for Mitch, but Lauren was devastated. Was she losing her soul mate? She felt confused and hurt, she didn't understand. She liked to focus on one thing, improving all the time. Lauren thought, *why didn't Mitch like to focus on one thing? Why doesn't he want to spend time with me? Doesn't he love me anymore? Was he lying to me?*

Mitch's desire for variety is an intrinsic element of who he is, and in time, Lauren came to this realisation. He is always looking for a new role to play. She learnt to value their shared running time, rather than resent the times she ran alone.

Spending time with Mitch was like being at a carnival. It was exhausting. Even on the rare occasions when they stayed in, his energy levels sucked the air out of the room. More and more Lauren found herself choosing to spend time apart. This worked for them both. Mitch could try new things and Lauren got some quiet time.

With his natural charm, Lauren wasn't surprised that Mitch liked to flirt. He was highly aware of and enjoyed his sexuality. His intoxicating presence was seductive, and he naturally developed many friends of both sexes. Often travelling, Mitch had a habit of making new friends in the departure lounge. The trouble was that many of these friends were seduced by his charm and had a different read on the relationship.

Mitch would claim to be shocked by their misinterpretation, but Lauren could see he secretly delighted in the attention. She began to feel she had been deceived. Mitch had made her the centre of his universe and now she felt deprived of his attention and betrayed by his behaviour. She could barely contain her jealousy. Despite Mitch's reassurance, she saw duplicity lurking in the shadows.

The longer they stayed together, the more Lauren understood Mitch's low tolerance for boredom and his desire to be attractive to others. If the relationship was to work, her attitude had to change. She took some time (*and a fair bit of therapy*) to work through her reaction, eventually realising this was part of Mitch. As long as they worked at keeping the excitement levels alive, Mitch always came home to her, not that it stopped him flirting. A sexually and mentally bored Mitch would feel compelled to look for fun elsewhere. For his part, Mitch learned that his enthusiasm to tell Lauren everything about every woman that he met was hurtful, so he reined it in a little.

One of Lauren's biggest gripes was Mitch's messiness. It was out of control. Towels were never hung up, empty toilet rolls flicked onto the bathroom floor, and bits of paper, from menus to business cards, were strewn everywhere. It did not enter his head to put the butter away or drop his clothes in the laundry basket. At first it was endearing—she was sure his habits would change when they lived together. They didn't.

Eventually, she got him to hang up his towel, but it was never the right way. When she returned home after a work trip away it was always to dishes piled up in the kitchen, a messy bathroom, and an unmade bed.

Despite Lauren's badgering and Mitch's promises to improve, nothing changed. With his high tolerance for nagging, Mitch laughs and whips her up in his arms, telling her he loves her. Having never had a high expectation of a perfect marriage, Mitch can't understand why these trivialities matter so much to Lauren. But they do, so they found a compromise. Mitch agreed to move his clothes from the floordrobe and into a holding bin—a place for clothes that are not ready for washing and may be worn again. Whenever Lauren was away, they hired a cleaner.

Mitch thinks out loud. He seems to be continually changing his mind, which Lauren finds infuriating, but his nature is to constantly question and redefine the world. For Lauren, life's rules are clearly set in concrete so increasingly she considers Mitch to be an airhead who needs to think more. The opposite is true. Mitch lives an open-ended life waiting for the best idea, the best opportunity, or the best solution.

When they argue, Mitch's anger quickly passes. He can move on and forget what's happened. Not so for Lauren who is left simmering and analysing what went wrong—often for days and sometimes weeks. Over the years, she has picked up some Mango traits, and instead of simmering for a week, she has reduced it to a day. After all, if Mitch isn't suffering, why should she?

When children came along, Mitch was the party parent. He's the dad who wakes the baby up to have fun, the dad who orders takeaway when Lauren's away or resorts to chips and party pies from the freezer. Mitch even kept the children home from school on occasions so they could spend the day together but only when Lauren was away. He cemented himself clearly in the role of good cop. It wasn't always fun being Mitch's kid though. With so many folders open simultaneously in his head, he would forget to drop them off at day care and arrive at work with the children sitting happily in the back seat. It goes without saying that he'd forgotten to pick them up after school. Several times.

Lauren is infuriated by Mitch's chronic lateness. He was late for birthday parties and football games and she hated that he let the kids down. She was embarrassed in front of the other parents and there were heated arguments that made no difference to Mitch's behaviour. In the end, Lauren planned everything for the children without including Mitch, and when he was there, it was a bonus.

There is a darker Mango side to Mitch when it comes to financial dexterity. His free-spirited attitude to life "we're here for a good time, not a long time," began to translate into tangible problems in the form of speeding fines, parking fines, and late payment fees.

When their year-old dishwasher broke, they couldn't claim warranty because Mitch had forgotten to complete the form online. Unperturbed, Mitch bought a new one. He saw himself as solving a problem and showing love—what a lovely surprise for Lauren. Instead, she was appalled at the lack of effort to fix it and the added expense.

Mitch had his own business by now, but it had been clear since early in their marriage that Lauren was more proficient at handling the family finances. More than that, she enjoyed it which was just as well, because if she'd had access to the business accounts, she would have noticed that Mitch's credit cards were always at their limit. She would have noticed his grand gestures of generosity: shouting rounds of champagne or picking up the dinner tab. Lovely in theory, perhaps, but if Lauren had known he had also financed two engagement rings for friends, she would have been horrified. He sometimes forgot to make the minimum payment each month, incurring late fees on top of soaring interest charges.

Mitch was aware of his spending habits, but he made excuses, including to himself. Ten years into their relationship, he had allowed his finances to get so out of hand even he was worried. He wanted to spare Lauren the burden of his debt, and knowing what happened the last time he was honest about all the women he met, he decided to keep it to himself. He wanted to chip away at the payments and get the balance down to show her how disciplined he was. She would be proud of him.

One night when they were at home alone after a lovely evening of cooking together and sharing future plans over a bottle of shiraz, Mitch thought he'd open up, get all the cards on the table. In a moment of what he now sees as pure lunacy, he revealed his debt to Lauren. Before he had a chance to proudly tell her how he was chipping away at it, Lauren turned white, then grey, then into a screaming maniac. The worst argument of their lives ensued, ending with Mitch walking out and staying with a friend for a week.

Lauren saw this as the ultimate betrayal. Mitch had lied to her and could never be trusted again. Everything Lauren had been saving for and working towards was a joke, as Mitch was eroding the family income without her knowledge. From Mitch's point of view, he had done nothing wrong— not intentionally. In fact, he was doing all he could to fix the problem, and he had been honest about it. He was shocked by Lauren's reaction. She asked him to leave, and he wasn't sure she would ever want him back.

Mitch did come home, but it was months before intimacy resumed and years before Lauren felt she could trust him again. It was the biggest hit, and the biggest test for their marriage. Although he will never lose his childlike wonder and love of fun, as he grew older, Mitch found it difficult to accept the aging process. He loves his beautiful, steady Lauren and thankful she's stayed with him though all his ups and downs.

Now into his fifties, Mitch still loves to have fun, but he has learnt that to have a secure future, which he's finally thinking about, he needs to manage his money. With Lauren's help, he regularly saves and gets his bills paid on time. But if you asked him if he regretted any of his earlier spending, he'd answer, 'Hell, no!'

Lauren shakes her head as she smiles lovingly at Mitch; her magnificent Mango.

Mango and Lime

For Limes, the Mango pull of being opposites is simply irresistible. They love the unselfconsciousness and freedom Mangoes have to be themselves. Mangoes love the wonderful calm and stability Limes can provide, and the way Limes keep them in line when their behaviour gets out of hand. With time and mutual respect, Mango will settle down, Limes will become more spontaneous, and they will meet happily somewhere near the middle.

Potential Problems

This combination can work like a dream, except in situations where Mango is overly impetuous and Lime is excessively possessive and parental. If a Lime can't bend the rules a little on how they live, Mango won't be able to cope. If Mango refuses to take anything seriously and stays a child forever, Lime may not hang around.

Mitch and Alyssa: the Mango and the Apple

Handsome Mitch swept Alyssa off her feet, despite her best efforts to resist. Working for a global telco, he travels most weeks but calls her regularly. That annoys her. She sees him as needy. He has made her the centre of his universe which she quite likes; it's what she deserves. He buys extravagant gifts, sends her flowers for no reason, and delights her with secrets and surprises. Alyssa doesn't have a great track record with men, and her friends tell her she has struck gold. Mitch cares about his appearance and going out with him by her side makes her feel good. He is magnetic company, charming her friends and attracting people with his enter-taining stories. The stories were a bit over the top, but she could cope. She felt they were a power couple. But Alyssa soon found that Mango and drama go hand in hand. Mitch has a flair for theatrics.

Mitch: You wouldn't believe it! This guy was after me and he was the size of three houses, full of muscle, and honestly more than 6 feet (190 centimetres) tall! I had no hope of escape … I was boxed in and I could feel the sweat streaming down my back, down my legs, until my socks were damp. His eyes locked on mine and I could hear him growl as he snarled and almost, took a lunge at me. Thank goodness for the security guards, who got to me just as he was close enough for me to smell the beer on his breath.

Mitch's world plays out in vibrant colour with characters painted big and bold. He doesn't live life on the sideline. He is always in the game where even the mundane becomes good theatre.

Garbage, Alyssa thought, and called it out. Smiling but without embarrassment, Mitch tells the real story. Alyssa doesn't let him get away with a thing. Even if he is convinced the orange is as big as a watermelon, she doesn't buy it for an instant. She's learned to ignore much of his exaggeration, laugh at some it, and get the facts when needed.

She likes that Mitch finds socialising so effortless. Alyssa was constantly challenged to find intelligent conversation in social situations, but Mitch made it much easier by providing a wider pool of friends to choose from.

When they married, Mitch was the perfect groom. Anything Alyssa wanted for her dream wedding, he made possible. She wanted a special location. He gave her a Scottish castle. She wanted unusual transport; he gave her six white horses and an 18th century carriage. She was quietly surprised at how much she liked the attention.

Like any extreme Mango, Mitch was a combination of actor and chameleon. With his desire to avoid sameness, he loves to try different activities. Alyssa was always up for a challenge, so she felt theirs was a marriage made in heaven.

She likes finding new challenges for them to conquer together. Alyssa works at a new skill until she's the best she can be, but by that time, Mitch is bored. They ran marathons, learnt to rock climb, and went to trivia nights where they were constantly on the winning team. And then Mitch stopped.

Like any couple who have been together for a while, the initial excitement and romance dimmed a little and Alyssa began to face the reality of life with Mitch the Mango. He talked all the time. And when she told a story, he had to top it with a better one. He talked over her when they were out, and even tried answering for her. Alyssa immediately made it very clear she was her own woman and would answer for herself.

Alyssa had misinterpreted Mitch's chameleon-like ability to change combined with his desire to try different things. She thought he liked all the things she did. He was sincere in his desire to make her happy and he loved a challenge, as long as it was different to the last challenge. Alyssa would have preferred Mitch continue with the activities she chose because she likes being with him, but it was never going to stay that way. Mitch's desire for variety is an intrinsic element of who he is. When Alyssa realised this, she learnt to value their time together and continued happily to achieve her own ambitious goals.

Being with Mitch is fun, but before long Alyssa tires of the constant socialising. She enjoys her own company, and often brings work home, so in time, they adjust their social lives to suit. Interestingly, Mitch begins choosing to stay home more with his headstrong Alyssa, even though it usually involves a bottle of wine.

With his natural charm, Alyssa is not surprised that Mitch likes to flirt. He is highly aware of and enjoys his sexuality, which is also a win for Alyssa. But his intoxicating presence is seductive to everyone and he naturally develops lots of friends of both sexes. He always meets new friends in the departure lounge, but many of them, seduced by his charm, read more into the relationship. Mitch claims to be shocked when his intentions are misinterpreted, but Alyssa can see he secretly delights in the attention.

She knew she would have to cut this behaviour off at the pass before it snowballed. Sitting Mitch down, she explained that he was leading women on, and if he chose to do that, she did she not want to hear about it. Alyssa added that if his behaviour went any further than innocent flirting, she would cut off the offending part of his anatomy and drop it in the blender. Mitch understood.

One of Alyssa's biggest gripes is Mitch's messiness. It is out-of-control. She couldn't believe a grown man dropped his clothes on the floor. Towels were never hung up, empty toilet rolls flicked onto the bathroom floor. Bits of paper, from menus to business cards, were strewn everywhere. It did not enter Mitch's head to put the butter away or drop his clothes in the laundry basket. At first it was endearing and Alyssa was sure that small habit would change when they lived together. It didn't. Once again, Alyssa read the riot act. She conceded some untidiness such as a glass left unwashed in the kitchen—only one glass—but not slobbery; not in her house. Mitch either pulled up his socks or they did not live together. As Mitch never takes anything seriously, he pretended to agree and gathered Alyssa up in his arms, telling her he loved her. Mitch doesn't have a high expectation of a perfect marriage and he can't understand why it matters. But it matters to Alyssa. She compromised a little, but Mitch learned she would not tolerate chaos. And there was something about this demanding, bossy woman he found damned attractive.

Mitch thinks out loud. He seems to be continually changing his mind, which Alyssa finds infuriating, but his nature is to constantly question and redefine information or circumstances. Alyssa see situations clearly and quickly, and increasingly considers Mitch as an airhead for not thinking things through. It's the opposite. Mitch lives an open-ended life waiting for the best idea, the best opportunity, and the best solution.

Their arguments were often one sided and fierce, but short lived. Mitch is more likely to give in, knowing it was probably his fault anyway, and if not, he doesn't really care. He has no desire to win. This, on its own, is enough to exacerbate Alyssa's frustration, but once her anger peters out, it's over and she moves on as quickly as Mitch.

When children come along, Mitch is the party parent. He's the dad who wakes up the baby to have fun, the dad who orders takeaway, or the dad who cooks chips and party pies from the freezer when Mum is away. Every night. Mitch keeps the children home from school at times so they can spend the day together but only when Alyssa is away. He has clearly cemented himself in the role of good cop. It isn't always fun being Mitch's kid. With so many folders open simultaneously in his head, Mitch forgets to drop them off at day care and arrives at work with the children happily sitting in the back seat. It goes without saying he's forgotten to pick them up after school. Several times.

Mitch's chronic lateness is unacceptable to Alyssa. He is late for birthday parties and football games. She considers it letting the kids down as selfish behaviour and poor parenting. She tells Mitch if it happens again, he will not be included in the children's celebrations and activities. Mitch is predictably sorry. Predictably he is late again. And predictably, Alyssa began to plan and attend all the children's events without telling Mitch and arranges someone else to collect the children from school. After a while, Mitch gets the message.

There is a darker side to Mango Mitch. His free-spirited approach to life, "we're here for a good time, not a long time", begins to translate into tangible problems in the form of speeding fines, parking tickets, and late payment fees.

When their year-old dishwasher breaks, they can't claim warranty because Mitch had forgotten to complete the form online. Unperturbed, Mitch buys a new one to solve the problem and show his love—what a lovely surprise for Alyssa. Instead, she is furious at the lack of effort to fix it and the added expense. She sends it back.

Although Mitch has his own business, it was clear early in their marriage that Alyssa was more proficient at handling the family finances. If she had had access to the business accounts, she would have noticed that Mitch's credit cards were always at the limit. She would have noticed the grand gestures of generosity: shouting rounds of champagne and picking up the tab for dinner. Lovely in theory perhaps, but if Alyssa had known Mitch had financed two engagement rings for friends, she would have cut up his cards on the spot. He sometimes forgets to make the minimum payment each month, incurring late fees on top of soaring interest charges.

Although Mitch is aware of his spending habits, he makes excuses, even to himself. Ten years into their relationship, he had let it get so out of hand now even he was worried. He doesn't want to burden Alyssa with his debt, and knowing what happened last time he was honest about all the women he met, he decides to keep it to himself and work on reducing the balance on his own. When he shows her how disciplined he is she will be proud of him.

One night, they were at home alone enjoying a lovely evening. They'd cooked together and were feeling close as they shared future plans over a bottle of shiraz. Mitch opens up, puts all his cards on the table and revealed his debt to Alyssa. It was a moment he now sees as pure lunacy. Before he has a chance to proudly tell her how he's chipping away at it, Alyssa turns icy and berates him like never before. The worst argument of their lives ensues.

In the morning, Alyssa sits Mitch down and demands to see all his business accounts and all his cards to understand his debt. Fortunately, the business is doing okay, despite Mitch's spending, and together they organise the debt to be consolidated into one loan. Mitch must show Alyssa the progress he's making each month. Alyssa is furious Mitch is wasting her time to fix his debt and is disappointed he didn't have the discipline to manage it himself. She loves him but has lost a level of respect.

From Mitch's point of view, he can't see he has done anything intentionally wrong. Sure, he had made errors and is now doing everything he can to fix the problem and he has been honest about it. He is upset at Alyssa's reaction but on reflection, realises he should have expected it. He doesn't mind being micromanaged because he loves Alyssa and he knows his spending was out of control. He is grateful she was there to help. Alyssa did regain her respect for Mitch, but only after the debt was reduced substantially. They now work towards their financial goals as a team.

Mitch will never lose his childlike wonder, but as he gets older, he finds it difficult to accept the aging process. He loves his rock Alyssa and thankful she has stayed with him though all the ups and downs. Now into his fifties, Mitch still loves to have fun, but he has learned after the credit card debacle to let Alyssa keep an eye on his books every quarter. These days, he only owns one credit card. But if you ask him if he regrets any of his earlier spending, he'll smile and answer, 'Hell, no!'

Alyssa rolls her eyes and shakes her head at Mitch, her magnificent Mango.

Mango and Apple

Mangoes accept criticism without taking it personally, and Apples are direct. If they give you loving criticism, it's a gift. Therefore, this couple tends to argue but both enjoy debate.

Challenges arise on which topics to debate: although both are conceptual, Apples want to talk about foreign affairs, politics, and business, but Mangoes only want to talk about those things if they focus on the people in the stories. Apples love the Mango playfulness that distracts them from their results-driven working mindset, and both connect on exciting physical pleasure. Mangoes love the diverse challenges an Apple partner brings and the fast pace at which they live life, and they both are impatient and frustrated by anything or anyone who slows them down.

Potential Problems

Mangoes can get impatient with Apples' constant quest for knowledge and can't imagine why they need a reason to do something—why not just enjoy life right now? They can feel like a child constantly berated by an overcontrolling parent and won't stick around if this continues. Apples can get frustrated with what they see as Mangoes' lack of depth and self-control, which they consider a weakness. Apples are not quick to forgive, if ever.

Mitch and Bella: the Mango and the Banana

Handsome Mitch swept Bella off her feet. Working for a global telco, he travels on a weekly basis but calls her regularly. She is the centre of his universe. He buys extravagant gifts, sends her flowers for no reason, and delights her with secrets and surprises. She is overwhelmed by the romance. Her friends tell her she has struck gold. Mitch cares about his appearance, and going out with him by her side makes her feel fantastic. He is irresistible company, charming her friends and attracting people to them with his entertaining stories. Bella soon found that Mango and Melodrama go hand in hand. Mitch has a flair for theatrics.

Mitch: You wouldn't believe it! This guy was after me and he was the size of three houses, full of muscle, and honestly more than 6 feet (190 centimetres) tall! I had no hope of escape … I was boxed in and I could feel the sweat streaming down my back, down my legs, until my socks were damp. His eyes locked on mine and I could hear him growl as he snarled and almost took a lunge at me. Thank goodness for the security guards, who got to me just as he was close enough for me to smell the beer on his breath.

Mitch's world plays out in vibrant colour, and the characters in it are painted big and bold. He doesn't live life on the sideline. He is always in the game where even the mundane can become good theatre.

Bella is upset to her core when she hears this story. Is Mitch alright? How terrifying it must have been! She can't wait to have him home safely so she can hug him. If Bella had been there to see it, she would have found the reality a little different. Bella is constantly amazed at Mitch's multi-hued stories that seem to get bigger and richer with each retelling. It's years before the rose-coloured glasses come off and she learns to distil much of his story—once she learned not to panic on Mitch's behalf and rush to his aid.

She loves that he finds socialising so effortless because she does too. But Mitch takes it to another level. For a while, her life is a whirlwind as he creates a pool of activities and friends to choose from.

When they get married, Mitch is the perfect groom. Whatever Bella wants for her dream wedding, he makes it happen. She wanted a special venue. He gave her a Scottish castle. She wanted unusual transport; he arranged six white horses and an 18th century carriage. She can't believe she has found her prince. They will live happily ever after.

Like any extreme Mango, Mitch is a combination of actor and chameleon. With his desire to avoid sameness, he loves trying different things. When Bella met Mitch, it was only natural she thought she'd won the lottery. He liked all the things she did. She loves spending time with her parents and siblings, and Mitch is happy to come along. She loves reading, he joins her book club. She takes up meditation, and he tags along. He will try anything, and his sense of freedom and lack of inhibition is intoxicating. Then, like any couple who've been together for a while, the initial excitement and romance dimmed a little and Bella began to face the reality of life with Mitch the Mango.

He talks all the time. When she has a story to tell, he tells a story that's one better. When they're out, he talks over her and even answers for her. 'Oh, sure, Bella would love that,' he would say when Bella is standing right there. It bugs her so she keeps talking to try and answer for herself, but often Mitch has moved the conversation along. She doesn't like it but she lets it go. Bella realises she has misinterpreted Mitch's chameleon-like ability to change combined with his desire to try different things. She thought he liked all the things she did. He was sincere in his desire to make her happy but seeing her family every weekend and staying in for quiet nights at home soon became boring. This is a natural progression for Mitch, but for Bella it's confusing. Never mind. She just wants to be with him. So, she does whatever Mitch suggests, from white water rafting, to weekends away, to trying every new bar and restaurant that opens.

While she loves his company, Bella begins to feel guilty about neglecting her family. She doesn't see them as often as she'd like. She feels guilty about her book club friends. They constantly hassle her for not turning up. She promises to catch up with all her friends but Mitch's activities keep her constantly busy.

Mitch's desire for variety is an intrinsic element of who he is. He is feeling irritated that he can't do anything on his own. Bella is always around. And she never says no. She says yes to everything and is starting to act needy. When he raises the issue, Bella doesn't defend herself. In time, Bella understands that this is simply who Mitch is and it is okay not to be with him every minute. She is disappointed he didn't stick with all the things she loves, but he does come along when there's something or someone new. Gradually they find their own space.

Being with Mitch is fun, but before long Bella is exhausted. Even on the rare occasions when they stay in, his energy sucks the air out of the room. More and more she finds herself choosing the times she goes out. This works for them both; Mitch can try new things and Bella has quiet time with family and friends.

With his natural charm, Bella isn't surprised that Mitch is a natural flirt. He is highly aware of and enjoys his sexuality, which is also a win for Bella. His intoxicating presence is seductive to everyone and he naturally develops friends of both sexes. He always has new friends he meets in the departure lounge. The trouble is, many of these new friends are seduced by his charm and read more into the relationship. Mitch claims to be shocked his intentions are misinterpreted, but Bella can see he is secretly delighted by the attention.

Bella is upset. She knows Mitch loves her—doesn't he? Hasn't he made her the centre of his universe? She talks to her friends about this over and over, twisting, analysing, and hypothesising. What should she do? Should she say something? If she does, he will accuse her of not trusting him, and she really did. In the end, she can't bear the thought of conflict, of him being angry with her, so she says nothing. Bella believes that because they don't argue, they have a happy and healthy relationship.

This is a common lie propagated by non-confrontational Bananas. She is damaging herself by internalising the issue and no relationship is nourished by lack of communication.

Professional counselling helps Bella raise this issue with Mitch in a non-aggressive, non-confrontational way. Even though he laughs it off, he can see that his behaviour has hurt his beloved Bella. She takes time to work through her concern and realises this is part of who Mitch is, and as long as she works at keeping excitement levels alive, Mitch will come home to her, although he will still flirt. For his part, Mitch has learnt that his compulsion and enthusiasm to tell Bella everything about every woman he meets is hurtful, so he reins it in, just a little.

Mitch's messiness is a problem. Towels are never hung

up, empty toilet rolls are flicked onto the bathroom floor, and bits of paper, from menus to business cards, are strewn everywhere. It doesn't enter Mitch's head to put the butter away or drop his clothes in the laundry basket. Bella has to admit Mitch's messiness is endearing. She doesn't mind picking up after him. The truth is, Bella didn't see the messiness straight away. For her the important thing was a happy, loving, and peaceful home, not one full of nagging and regulation.

Mitch thinks out loud. He seems to continually change his mind which Bella finds confusing at first, but his nature is to constantly question and redefine things. She loves his insatiable curiosity and excitement about the world and wishes she was more like him. Mitch lives an open-ended life waiting for the best idea, the best opportunity, and the best solution. Neither one of them likes to argue and when they do it's usually instigated by Mitch when his quick wit turns to nasty sarcasm. Bella ends up hurt but Mitch's anger quickly passes. He soon has her laughing again although the hurt can take longer to heal.

When children come along, Mitch is the party parent. He's the dad who wakes up the baby to have fun, the dad who orders take away or heats up chips and party pies from the freezer when Bella is away. Mitch even keeps the children home from school at times so they can spend the day together. Bella loves the relationship Mitch has with the children and is occasionally convinced to take a day off with them. These are her favourite times, and Mitch has clearly cemented himself in the role of good cop.

It wasn't always fun being Mitch's kid though. With so many folders open simultaneously in his head, he will forget to drop them off and arrive at work with the children happily sitting in the back seat. It goes without saying he forgets to pick them up. Often.

Mitch suffers from chronic lateness. When it impacts their children, Bella is upset for them. He is late for birthday parties and football games. She reminds him, and he continues to forget. She hates to nag but after a while she didn't have to. She leaves it up to the children. When they asked him repeatedly why he missed their games, Mitch started to change. He may never have been early, but he was better.

There was a darker side to Mango Mitch though. His free-spirited approach to life, 'we're here for a good time, not a long time,' began to translate into tangible problems in the form of speeding fines, parking tickets, and late payment fees.

When their year-old dishwasher broke, they couldn't claim warranty because Mitch had forgotten to complete the form online. Unperturbed, Mitch bought a new one. He was solving a problem and showing his love, and what a lovely surprise for Bella. She was delighted but wished they didn't have to spend the money.

It had become fairly clear in their marriage that neither Mitch or Bella particularly enjoyed handling the family finances. Mitch ended up with the responsibility because Bella was so laid back and relaxed about it. Big mistake.

Bella had no idea how fiscally deficient Mitch could be. He had his own business now, so she assumed that he was managing money well. But if she'd had access to the business accounts, she would have noticed that Mitch's credit cards were always at the limit. She would have noticed the grand gestures of generosity: rounds of champagne and picking up the tab for dinner. Lovely in theory perhaps, but if Bella had known he had also financed two engagement rings for friends she would have been somewhat concerned he was giving away the family farm. He sometimes forgot to make the minimum payment each month, incurring late fees on top of soaring interest costs.

Mitch was aware of his spending habits, but he made excuses—even to himself. Ten years into their relationship, he had let it get so out of hand and even he was getting worried. He didn't want Bella to bear the burden of his debt and, knowing what happened last time he was honest about all the women he met, he decided to keep it to himself. He would pay the balances down and show her how disciplined he was. She would be proud of him.

One night they were home alone enjoying a lovely evening. They'd cooked together and were feeling close as they shared future plans over a bottle of shiraz. In a spontaneous effort to share the load of his worry, Mitch opens up and reveals his debt to Bella.

Bella gasps. She feels ill. She has worked hard and made sure to contribute to their savings every week. What Mitch has told her will put their plans back by years. Mitch keeps talking, explaining, reasoning, until she quietly retreats into herself and hears nothing but white noise. As she slowly returns to the conversation, she knows there is no point being angry. After all, it's done. Mitch feels an enormous sense of relief at sharing the problem, knowing Bella would be by his side to help fix it. Together they work out a plan to make their way out of debt.

Although Mitch will never lose his childlike wonder of the

world, as he grows older, he finds it more difficult to accept the aging process. He loves his beautiful, steady Bella and is thankful she's stayed with him though all their ups and downs. Now in his fifties, Mitch still loves to have fun, but has learnt that to have some stability in the future, which he's finally thinking about—he needs to manage his money better. With the credit card debacle behind them, he spends less, but his spending patterns don't change and his business swings constantly in and out of debt.

Bella has learned to keep the family finances separate. Now the children are through school, she checks up on Mitch regularly and is always assured that everything is fine. Besides, she still enjoys those luxury holidays he organises. They might be having a great time in their fifties, but Mitch and Bella will be working well into their seventies because of their lack of disciplined saving. If you ask Mitch if he regrets any of his spending earlier on, he'll answer, 'Hell, no!'

Bella smiles adoringly as she shakes her head at her magnificent Mango Mitch.

Mango and Banana

Mangoes and Bananas both love people and can connect through their shared respect of healthy relationships and ability to talk freely about their feelings.

At first, the pace and passion is intoxicating to the Banana, who loves the Mango confidence and all the romance and fun they create around sex. They love the way the Mango introduces them to all sorts of experiences they may never have sought out.

Mangoes love the Banana adoration and the way they

place them on a pedestal and seem to anticipate their every need. They are appreciative of this bottomless well of love, which makes them feel grounded and validated.

Potential Problems

Watch for Mangoes becoming bored with the Banana's desire for peace and quiet and to do good in the community. Mango prefers to have the focus on themselves. Mango energy levels can be exhausting for Banana partners, who need to take things more quietly. If the pace never slows, Bananas may consider giving up. Mangoes can become impatient with Banana's desire for a quieter life, their excessive detail in conversation, and the fact that they are just so damned nice.

Mitch and Mel: the Double Mango

Handsome Mitch swept Mel off her feet. Working for a global telco, he travels on a weekly basis but calls her regularly. He makes her the centre of his universe. He buys extravagant gifts, sends flowers for no reason, and delights her with secrets and surprises. Her friends tell her she has struck gold. Mitch is super stylish, as she is, and when they are out together, she feels like she can take on the world. She can't believe how alike they are. Mitch is irresistible company, charming her friends and attracting people to them with his limitless stories of playing golf and dining out with celebrities. She loves a good story! It was no surprise to Mel to discover with Mitch that his flair for theatrics and drama go hand in hand.

Mitch: You wouldn't believe it! This guy was after me and he was the size of three houses, full of muscle, and honestly more than 6 feet (190 centimetres) tall! I had no hope of escape ... I was boxed in and I could feel the sweat streaming down my back, down my legs, until my socks were damp. His eyes locked on mine and I could hear him growl as he snarled and almost took a lunge at me. Thank goodness for the security guards, who got to me just as he was close enough for me to smell the beer on his breath.

How lucky was Mitch to get away? And so brave! Thinks Mel.

Mel: When Mitch called, I could barely hear him. His voice was ragged ... I couldn't believe it was him. You can imagine the panic I went into. He is so strong and fit but with several guys on him, he could have been killed ...

That story dominated their dinner parties for months even though the true story was far less dramatic. Mitch's world plays out in vibrant colour, and the characters in it are painted big and bold. He doesn't live life on the sideline. He is always in the game where even the mundane becomes good theatre, with Mel is by his side, matching his stories and his laughs.

They live a whirlwind social life and Mel is happy to keep pace. Over time though, it becomes clear that they are often competing for airspace, particularly when they have an audience. For the first time in her life, Mel has learnt to pull back and give Mitch the stage. After all, he was never going to give that up—it seems he might be the bigger Mango.

When they marry, Mitch is the perfect groom. Whatever Mel want for her dream wedding, he makes it happen. She wanted a special venue. He gives her a Scottish castle. She wanted unusual transport. He provides her six white horses and an 18th century carriage. And when she demanded bagpipes, a gospel choir, fireworks, and 2,000 tiny pearls sewn into her gown, she got that too.

Like any extreme Mango, Mitch was a combination of actor and chameleon. With his desire to avoid sameness, he loves trying different things. So, when Mel met Mitch, it was only natural she thought she'd won the lottery. He likes anything she does. Parties, dancing, running, fine dining. Whatever he hasn't tried, he tries. His sense of freedom and lack of inhibition was intoxicating. Then, like any couple who've been together for a while, the initial excitement and romance dims a little and Mel begins to face the reality of life with her Mango double.

He talks all the time, and every time she tells a story, he tells a better one! When they're out, he talks over her, and once tried answering for her. Well that wasn't going to last! Many heated discussions later, Mitch clicked. He had to make some sort of effort to change. Not that he ever succeeded.

Mel had misinterpreted Mitch's chameleon-like ability to change combined with his desire to try different things. She thought he liked all the things she did. She demands attention and is a little put out when he wants to do different things. It's not a matter of something new every time, it was more about variety. Had Mel closely considered this quality, she would have recognised herself. But like Mitch, she is too self-absorbed and too independent to follow him into new ventures. They settled on a mix of finding activities to do together and maintaining their individual schedules of excitement.

Being with Mitch was constantly fun. Whatever she suggested, he said yes, and she always said yes to his crazy ideas. They dined out together, sampling different restaurants on their way home. When one travelled for work, the other tried to meet up for a weekend away before or after.

With his natural charm, Mel wasn't surprised that Mitch liked to flirt. He was highly aware of and enjoyed his sexuality, a win-win as far as Mel was concerned. But his intoxicating presence was seductive to everyone and he naturally developed friends of both sexes. He always had new friends he'd met in the departure lounge. The trouble was that many of these friends were seduced by his charm, reading more into the relationship. Mitch claimed to be shocked his intentions were misinterpreted, but Mel could see he secretly delighted in the attention.

Mel is completely confident she can keep Mitch by her side. She finds it amusing that other women want her man and can't have him. She's not jealous, but she doesn't need him to endlessly tell her about the women he meets so Mitch agrees to tone it down a little. Mel is also an outrageous flirt, but she's not silly enough to tell Mitch. The Mango-Mango relationship is sexually rock solid, so there is no reason for either to stray. They understand each other perfectly.

Mitch's messy household habits are out of control. Towels are never hung up, empty toilet rolls are flicked onto the bathroom floor, and bits of paper, from menus to business cards, are strewn everywhere. It doesn't enter Mitch's head to put the butter away or drop his clothes in the laundry basket. This became a problem. With a penchant for beautiful things, Mel had spent a lot of money furnishing her apartment, and before Mitch moved in, it always looked good (ok, maybe never perfect but she gave it a good try). Now it was a constant battle to keep any order at all. Mel will never be anyone's housekeeper, so they paid a professional to clean and tidy weekly.

With a constant drive to question and redefine, Mitch and Mel both think out loud and live an open-ended life waiting for the best idea, the best opportunity, or the best solution. This means there's a lot of talking and not much listening. One will suggest and the other thinks it's a plan. The other one has forgotten it within minutes and made alternate plans. They had to constantly regroup to make sure their plans were in synch. Soon enough, one would be distracted, and they'd forget what they were excited about in the first place. Their friends think it's hilarious.

When they argue, they often forgot what the argument was about, and it was usually over quickly. Mel's mother once reminded her of the argument she and Mitch had over the car last September, but Mel was puzzled. She had deleted that folder soon after the argument ended.

When children came along, Mitch was the party parent. He's the dad who wakes up the baby to have fun. The dad who orders takeaway or heats up chips and party pies from the freezer when Mel was away. Mitch even keeps the children home from school at times so they could spend the day together. But only when Mel is away. He has clearly cemented himself in the role of good cop.

But with children came real, adult responsibility and it was impossible for both Mitch and Mel to continue their carefree existence. Now they had nappies, immunisations, day care, teething, sleepless nights, homework, playdates, and school fees to think about. If they had to measure their Mangoness, Mitch was 10/10 so it was up to Mel, a solid 8/10, to dip into her second preference and find order and organisation in her inner Lime. At times she resented being the bad cop, but clearly there was no other choice.

It wasn't always fun being Mitch's kid. With so many folders open simultaneously in his head, he would forget to drop them off at day care and arrive at work with the children happily sitting in the back seat. It goes without saying that he'd forget to pick them up. Several times.

Mitch was chronically late, and punctuality wasn't Mel's strength either. Since becoming a mother, she had improved but still often arrived in the nick of time to birthday parties and football games. Mitch was always late—often so late he would miss most of the event. Poor kids! And they loved their dad so much. Mel used the same trick she used on herself— she lied. She gave Mitch a time half an hour earlier so they would be on time and keep everybody happy.

Mitch's free-spirited approach to life, 'we're here for a good time, not a long time,' began to translate into tangible problems in the form of speeding fines, parking tickets, and late payment fees.

When their year-old dishwasher broke, they couldn't claim warranty because Mitch had forgotten to complete the form online. Unperturbed, he bought a new one. He was solving a problem and showing his love for Mel, and she was fine with it. She just wanted a dishwasher that worked.

Early in their marriage it became obvious that neither one of them was interested in life's trivialities, administration, or the paying of bills. Occasionally bills were paid on time, mostly they were late and incurred fees. Unfortunately, neither Mitch or Mel was overly motivated by money. They enjoyed it when it was there, but when times were tight, such as when Mitch was made redundant, they lived off less and invented cheaper ways to have fun.

However, Mitch now had his own business and he was getting himself into trouble. His credit cards were always at the limit thanks to his grand gestures of generosity shouting rounds of champagne or picking up the dinner tab. He loved throwing money around, but he wished his friends hadn't come to him when they needed engagement rings or short-term loans or, in the case of one friend, to be bailed out of a failing business.

Mitch is aware of his spending habits, but he makes excuses, even to himself. Ten years into their relationship, he had let it get so out of hand even *he* was worried. He didn't want Mel to bear the burden of his debt; he kept it to himself and worked at paying off the cards. He would show her how disciplined he was and she'd be proud of him. One night they were home alone enjoying a lovely evening. They'd cooked together and were talking big Mango plans over a bottle of shiraz. Mitch decided to open up, get all the cards on the table, and reveal his debt to Mel.

They had children now and Mel tried to be understanding. The debt was unexpected, and it put them behind the eight ball. It certainly stopped the evening in its tracks. After a biting rant, Mel took herself off to bed. The following morning, she had moved on. It was done, and now they would fix it.

There would be no ski trip this year and she would find a way to ensure Mitch made up for his fiscal mismanagement.

From Mitch's point of view, he had done nothing wrong intentionally. He had made errors and now he was doing all he could to fix the problem. And he had been honest about it. Sure, he felt bad, but nothing that couldn't be fixed, right? After all, no-one died.

Although Mitch will never lose his childlike wonder of the world, as he grew older both he and Mel struggled to accept the aging process. They are thankful for each other and cosmetic surgery.

Now in his fifties, Mitch still loves to have fun, but has learnt that to have a secure future, which he's finally thinking about—he needs to better manage his money. Together with Mel they pay their bills on time, deal with administrative tasks, and even put away some savings. But if you asked him if he regrets any of his earlier spending, he'll answer, 'Hell, no!'

The last we heard, Mitch and Mel had sold their house and were living in Nicaragua.

Double Mango

When two Mangoes team up, they must take turns to be the centre of attention. It's handy to have a couple of Mangoes at dinner parties because they will fill any awkward gaps in conversation and entertain other guests. They share a childlike ability to have fun and experience new challenges, so tend to attack their interests with equal passion. They enjoy each other's capacity to be nimble, make quick decisions, and spend money on anything new and interesting. Their challenge is to survive the fast and frantic pace without exhausting each other. Listening becomes a valuable skill between two people who would prefer to talk—if they don't learn to listen, they will fall into the trap of each feeling their own needs are not being met.

Potential Problems

Two Mangoes will create a fun household with high levels of energy, but they will often compete to be the most fabulous. Often the bigger, juicier Mango will win out with the other reluctantly playing second fiddle. With their substantial egos, and continued need for approval and recognition, two Mangoes can clash.

At some point, one will have to assume responsibility for paying bills, filling out forms, and organising tradesmen or find a good personal assistant. Often the more moderate Mango will find themselves dipping in to their secondary or even third preference, wearing their Lime hat more and more often. To sustain this double Mango relationship, one will need to put aside any resentment and be prepared to step out of the spotlight. And that's the challenge.

How to handle the Mango in your life

When you hear a story that could impact others, make sure you drill down for details. It's easy to come unstuck going head to head with someone over a traffic incident, only to find your Mango may have been the one at fault.

Not everything your Mango says can be taken as gospel or as a problem that needs solving. Mangoes think out loud and solve problems best by talking them through. This doesn't necessarily mean you need to contribute; pay attention to see if they're they looking for advice or simply verbalising their options.

Because they're passionate by nature, you may find your Mango makes strong statements that can be hurtful. Days later when you raise how upset you were, they don't recall what they said. They tend to say so much in such a limited amount of time they can be shocked that they caused offence. When they say something that bothers you, ask yourself if it was said flippantly or whether it was meant to cut. Mangoes rarely intend to wound, so tell them when they do. Try not to hold a grudge; they never will.

Whatever you're upset about, don't expect the self-absorbed Mango to notice. You will need to bring the issue to their attention. The beauty of this is they don't take too much to heart and are open to feedback; that's if you can manage to make them take your feedback seriously.

Mangoes are not great listeners. They will try, but the reality is that they live life like puppies being let on the grass for the first time. When you need their attention, you must instruct them to listen.

Mangoes are great socialisers and will help if being social doesn't come naturally to you, but they will eventually expect you to handle matters yourself. They need to know they're free to mingle and spread their love around without needing to babysit you.

Banish jealousy. An unproductive emotion at the best of times, jealousy will destroy you when you're with a Mango. They are charming and likeable and will always have plenty of fans.

Try not to stifle their ideas before they've had time to

finish their sentence. Many people grow tired of hearing the constant stream of big ideas, so they shut them down before their idea is out. Your Mango will be crushed, and over time, will become resentful.

Be confident that once a Mango is committed to you, they will settle down. If you want to survive this relationship, you need to be flexible around their many interests, but don't feel you must buy into everything they do. Extreme Mangoes have a high tolerance for drugs, alcohol, challenge, and risk. Let them forge new frontiers while you take a quiet break from Mango madness.

In a Mango relationship you will need to be the responsible partner. Be realistic about their ability with money. Handle the finances yourself, double-check theirs, and remind them to keep track of responsibilities. Find a compromise between smothering Mango's spontaneity and allowing them to get away with whatever they try on. On a hot summer's night, head to the beach for fish and chips rather than splurging at the fine dining restaurant. Don't begrudge their toys or try to continually rein them in. You were originally attracted to their passion, spontaneity, and genuine love of life, so let them share these experiences with you. Just enjoy it.

Tips for Mangoes

When you've achieved something at home, congratulate yourself. You don't need recognition from your partner to say the house looks tidy, the cake tastes great, or well done on bringing in the washing. Everyone knows what a bloody legend you are, but it can be tedious to be expected to say it repeatedly.

Work on a bit of self-control. Next time you are about to act on impulse, stop and ask yourself, *Will it affect the household in any way?* Try planning. I know, crazy thought. But when you have a job to do, stop and write down the steps you need to accomplish to achieve a result. This will allow you to see any flaws in your plan and may prevent impulsive behaviour, possibly saving you time and money in the long run.

Add some healthy worry to your life. Each time you do something that involves risk, think of what could go wrong. This doesn't mean you stop doing it. This just means you may make a better decision if you take time to consider the implications. Safeguard yourself against yourself. Worry about your partner. Watch the decisions you make and note how those decisions may have put them at risk. Spend some time thinking about what's important to them. Empathy alert!

Understand that your tendency to laugh when things are bad and not take problems seriously can irritate your partner. Learn when to lighten problems with laughter and when empathy is a more appropriate response.

Try not to talk at the same time as someone else, raise your voice to talk over them, or finish their sentences. These traits are irritating, even to other Mangoes. Once you have finished a point, pause and allow the other person to get a word in.

When they tell you a story, don't immediately follow up with a similar, better story about you. You may think you're exhibiting empathy, but this behaviour demonstrates self-absorption by bringing the conversation back to you. When you're telling an important story, stick to the facts and don't jump all over the place. You know you're prone to a little exaggeration.

Remember your charm. People from all walks of life fall for you with ease, and while you may have the best intentions, realise you become bored and tend to move on. This applies to new friends as well as lovers, who feel betrayed and are left with the impression that you are shallow and fickle.

Understand that other people's feelings may be more sensitive than yours. Be aware that you may be leading them on. What you see as friendly, they see as flirtatious.

Don't say "I love you" to everyone all the time. Think about those words as a precious resource to be used accordingly.

Short and Sweet

Mangoes in a relationship

- disorganised
- fun, fast, and social
- spendthrift
- generous and extravagant with gifts
- will put you on a pedestal
- poor time management
- don't argue much
- forgive and forget quickly
- always trying new things.

Mango Sticking points

- lose track of the facts
- lose interest easily in common activities
- flirtatious and surrounded by admirers
- messy at home
- don't take things seriously
- bad at financial control.

Mixed Fruit

Mango-Lime: the most common pairing. Mangoes love the calmness and stability of a Lime, and Limes love Mango's freedom and lack of inhibition. Mangoes get frustrated with too many rules, and Limes with lack of respect for rules.

Mango-Apple: no-one takes anything too personally. Mangoes love the challenges, pace, and intellect. Apples love the playfulness. Mangoes get frustrated with Apples' lecturing and quest for knowledge, and Apples with Mangoes' lack of depth and self-control.

Mango-Banana: both love people. Mangoes love the adoration and unconditional love, Bananas love Mangoes' confidence and freedom. Mangoes get bored with Bananas' desire for peace, and Bananas find Mangoes exhausting.

Double Mangoes: both share a sense of fun, energy, and a love of hedonistic pleasures. To have a successful relationship, one will have to step down from centre stage and become responsible for life's necessary detail.

Handling a Mango

- get the details when it's necessary
- talk big picture
- don't take everything they say out loud as gospel
- be capable of handling yourself socially without their back up
- don't try and keep up
- enjoy their passion and zest for life
- banish jealousy
- take responsibility for the admin in life
- keep sex interesting
- don't crowd them
- tell them when you're upset
- don't bother nagging, it doesn't work
- don't stew over an argument—they've forgotten as soon as it's over.

Tips for Mangoes

- pat yourself on the back without needing others to do it
- work on self-control
- try planning
- don't talk over people
- don't always dominate the conversation
- don't always have a story about you
- know when you can bend the truth and when you must have the facts
- be sensitive to others' feelings
- worry about the risks you take for yourself and your partner
- know when it's appropriate to laugh and when it's not.

Chapter 9

Loving Limes

I aspire to Lime perfection in my home. They're the ones whose homes come straight from the pages of *Vogue Living*. Creative Limes often have a sense of style which, combined with their economic values, means a neat and well-presented home tastefully decorated that didn't cost the earth.

Limes are fastidious housekeepers. Not only through their sense of order but also their sense of duty. They feel an obligation to keep their lives in good shape, unlike the rest of us. And because we know Limes will take care of the mundane, we don't need to!

It's a mystery to me why a dear friend spends so much time ensuring her house looks pristine each day when she's not expecting guests. Floors are swept, beds made, cushions plumped, and sinks scrubbed. When Limes clean the house, they follow a well thought out method. Limes will work through each room with logical precision and cannot rest until the job is done.

No doubt any Limes reading this definition are puzzled. They don't see any other option. I want the Lime's house but I don't want to do the work.

If you live with a Lime, you'll know they like to keep things. For a long time. Limes are hoarders in the nicest possible way. They never throw out any item that can be used or might possibly be used in the future. That's why my dad still has the heater he won for salesman of the year at Johnson & Johnson in 1965. Yes, you got it folks—1965. And it still works. So why would you get rid of it?

To be truthful, I am a touch Lime deficient, which is a shame because I come from a Lime-leaning family. I was helping my parents out at their church fête a while back, and there was one of my handbags—one I had thrown out, eighteen years earlier. My mother takes such good care of her bags they never pass their use by date. Each night they are cleaned out and stored in soft covers.

Go hunting in a Lime garage and you'll find old school papers and love letters that date back for decades. The combination of being financially responsible (overspending gives them heart palpitations), quietly sentimental, and a desire for consistency means you'll need a really big garage if you're married to a Lime.

My sister and I are six years apart, so as a child, I didn't notice her Lime tendencies. As an adult, she is the responsible one who keeps a check on me. When I spend a little too much on a slice of French brie, I remember not to tell her.

My mum had a major birthday a while back and my sister and I decided to give her friends a taste of India. I decided we would cook and managed to convince her it would be fun—a labour of love. I planned a fabulous theme and chose a vast and expensive menu. Jen consulted hire companies, toned down the menu, and added practical yet acceptable decorations. She also remembered to work with my Apple side and ran all changes past me, so I thought I was in control. But we all know she was running the show. The same sister had a run sheet for her wedding ceremony. Arrive church: 16:53 hours. Top of aisle: 16:59 hours. Begin aisle walk: 17:00 hours. Limes make terrific event planners.

Limes are expert managers of the household budget.

My dad always did the grocery shopping in our family. Being a good Lime, he shops carefully and patiently, reading labels for nutrition and looking for specials. It does take a while though. I could drop Dad at the supermarket on Saturday and come back on Tuesday, and he would just be finishing up. When my dad and his fellow Limes are grocery shopping, you can guarantee they have read all the catalogues and know the 2 litre fruit juice is on special. I doubt he would survive a shopping experience with me. Products fly off the shelves and crash into the trolley, regardless of price. When no-one's looking, I ride the trolley like a skateboard down the aisle. When you see someone doing that, give that Mango a smile.

Limes buy petrol on a Tuesday because that's when prices are lowest and they always use their discount fuel dockets. A Lime was telling me that when he had to tighten his belt recently, he did an inventory of the pantry and freezer to work out how long they could last on the existing food. Impressive! But sometimes, Limes are so careful with their planning, spending, and saving, they forget to live life in the moment.

You are very lucky to have a Lime partner who will quietly and efficiently run your household for you. Remember to notice their efforts and thank them. You may not have impromptu parties or receive roses every week, but you will have the best and most efficient rainwater tank in the street and your insurance payments will always be up to date.

Socially, Limes can come across as cool and aloof, which may confuse the person chasing them. Typically, **they are shy and cautious** about revealing too much of themselves. Limes don't jump into any type of relationship; instead, they will seal off their emotions until they're confident it's fine to move ahead. Once in a familiar environment, you will be surprised by how they shine.

Limes may only speak when they have something worth saying, but wait until they get the floor in a social situation. Suddenly excited that everyone has else has finally shut up and they have an opportunity to talk about their passion, a Lime's enthusiasm is like an oil spill that can't be contained. In small groups, they are confident with topics they love.

There's a myth that Limes hate surprises. They love surprises, as long as they can plan them. Not only must you believe it, but it's important to respect it. Never do the pop-in with your Lime friends.

My friend Mike arrived home one night with a fragrant bunch of lilies for his Lime partner Lily. That was his thing— beautiful lilies for beautiful Lily. He knew she'd been working hard and perhaps he hadn't been pulling his weight around the house as he should. Here's how it went:

'Surprise, sweetheart!' Mike said as he wrapped his arms around her from behind.

Lily disentangled herself from his hold, thinking, *can't he see I'm peeling carrots?*

'What are these for?' Lily asked.

'Beautiful lilies for my beautiful Lily!'

'Well, I'm going to Melbourne on Monday for a week, so I won't be here to enjoy them. But I hope you do.'

Poor old Mike. Well meant, but badly planned. Lily knows everything she's doing over the next month. Not only was the gift of flowers poorly timed, she will now worry that Mike has wasted money. There is no way the lilies will open before Monday. Perhaps she will give them to her mother.

Limes dislike unpredictability in their lives. Unpredictability disrupts the order and the harmony of a Lime's carefully planned day. They like to be prepared for all options. That's why when you have a headache, they have painkillers in their bag. When it rains, they never forget their umbrella, and when you break a nail, they have a file.

The Lime world is dictated by black and white rules and doing the right thing, guided by their own strong moral principles. They hate letting emotions and urges win. The stronger the Lime preference, the harder it would be to stay in bed, make love once more, and be late for work. Because they are ruled by "Should Do," it's almost impossible for Limes to forgive themselves when they try a "Would Like To Do". They don't operate on instinct so when it comes to making decisions, all they can do is weigh up which is the right thing to do.

Limes take responsibility for the moral code of conduct in the house and try to instil their sure sense of the right thing in their partners. When they don't measure up to their own high standards, they suffer remorse and often shame which can fill their heads for days, sometimes weeks—long after you've forgotten. Your loyal and dependable Lime will provide a haven of calm, harmony, and efficiency. What a gift.

A Lime story in four different flavours

This is the tale of Liam, **whose first behavioural preference is extreme Lime**. And here are the stories of what could happen depending on which Fruit he pairs with.

Liam and Alex: the Lime and the Apple

When Liam started looking for a partner, he did so with the seriousness with which he approached everything else in his life. It was typically methodical because to choose wrongly would mean making a mistake. That would mean embarrassment, which Liam avoided at all costs. Once he had determined the criteria for his perfect partner, he registered his profile on an internet dating app. This was the perfect medium for him to vet potential lovers with maximum efficiency. After several trials, he met Alex who worked at a pharmaceutical company, and slowly romance blossomed. But Liam didn't trust easily. A sensitive soul, he kept a carefully built wall around his emotions, afraid to be hurt and let down.

At first, Alex took this for aloofness and lack of commitment, but as they got to know each other, he realised it was simply Liam's reserved style. Used to being on his guard, Liam sometimes slowed things down himself by misinterpreting signs when Alex had no hidden agenda. Because Limes are such great observers of human nature, they tend to think others are studying them with equal intensity. He resisted for some time, but finally relented and let Alex move in. First into his head, then into his heart and finally into his home.

Liam treasured his home. Over the years, he had carefully cultivated designer pieces from all over the world. As an interior designer, Liam's sense of beauty and harmony was showcased in a seamless, tranquil environment. When Alex first moved in, Liam was anxious. His possessions were of the utmost importance. The carefully selected pieces—the Philippe Starck, for heaven's sake! The artwork! Then there were his clothes—ironed, hung up, and categorised by colour. What if Alex didn't show the same respect to his things that he did? His fears were unfounded. Alex wasn't quite as enthusiastic about his own clothes, but he understood Liam's desire to cherish his possessions, and was proud of the home Liam had created.

With Alex in his life, Liam now spent more time in his beautiful home. He always liked being at home alone but found he really enjoyed the predictability of a long-term relationship. He started planning their evening meals and leaving work earlier to come home and prepare them. Liam enjoyed a love of food and wanted to share his passion. Alex worked out a lot and was specific about his diet. Liam was only too happy to create new ideas around fresh, healthy food, and Alex was only too happy to eat it. Everybody wins.

Liam continued to look after the running of the house. He compiled a list of chores to do each day, divided into daily and weekly tasks. He expected that each chore should be highlighted in green when they were completed. The household budget, along with the wine collection, was detailed on a spreadsheet. He didn't have a cleaner because they didn't do it properly and he preferred to clean his own house—to perfection.

Alex was okay with this. He thought it was kind of sweet that Liam had this organisation thing down pat although he didn't really adhere to it. He ignored the direction on highlighter pens, but couldn't deny the logic of an efficient system, so went along with Liam's household rules, breaking them whenever he felt like it.

This was a source of stress for Liam, who expected Alex to complete his assigned jobs with accuracy and competence. There was a "right" way to do everything, and those of you who've ever stacked a Lime's dishwasher incorrectly will know what I mean. In the fridge and the pantry there is a place for everything. Knives must face a certain direction in the drawer. Books must be arranged in either alphabetical order, categories, or Liam's preference: colour coding. But never mix the methods. Alex found all this charming, and loved the organisation that Liam bought into his home, all the time doing things his own way.

Liam continued to manage the household affairs and Alex was happy as long as he didn't have to deal with the detail. But when he saw the amounts Liam was paying for insurance, every damned insurance you could think of—household, car, life, income protection, funeral, travel, flood, fire, health, long term care, liability insurance—he lost it. They were completely over insured, and the money was wasted. He demanded Liam cut back, and after much analysis and agonising, Liam agreed.

An important part of Alex's social life is his old university friends—a group that had expanded as they married and settled down. They tried to get together every weekend and often went away in large groups. While Liam was confident in small groups of people he knew, he constantly felt uncomfortable in Alex's group. He was a good listener, but even good listeners become bored and frustrated when they're not asked any questions. Liam has always been quick to like and dislike and knew from the beginning that this group wasn't for him.

All of Alex's friends worked in pharmaceuticals and they constantly talked shop, which was limiting for Liam. He felt they breached courtesy standards by sticking to topics which excluded him. After a while, Liam refused to be part of these dinners. He considered separate activities and groups of friends to be healthy for a relationship, but not when the friends make up the bulk of your partner's social circle. Alex was unrepentant and thought Liam was being too sensitive, and Liam was upset and stressed and refused to be subjected to dinners where he felt inadequate, despite being an expert in his own field.

They argued a lot over this. Liam found Alex quite provocative when he argued. He almost seemed to get a power surge from it, whereas all Liam felt was a power failure. Alex needed to win, and Liam would not budge an inch. The argument always ended with Liam retreating to build up his next case, not wanting to say the wrong thing, lose control, and be embarrassed. His argument was dominated by what Alex's friends should do. He couldn't see why they had to break the rules of social interaction. He focused on what he saw as their mistakes. In the end, the only way to get any clarity around this was compromise. Both having logical minds, they could see that it would be unreasonable for Alex to give up his long-term friends. They could also see it was unreasonable to ask Liam to sit through these dinners every week.

So, after a week or two of Liam's silent treatment, they agreed that Alex would cut back on seeing his friends as much as he did, from weekly to fortnightly. Liam wouldn't attend every event, perhaps see them once a month and make an effort (begrudgingly) to be less sensitive.

Alex thought Liam's slow decision-making process would drive him crazy. When they needed to get a plumber in, Liam researched the existing problem, assessing ways it could be fixed, looked for plumbers, interviewed them, and analysed who would provide the best value. He won't touch a problem until every alternative has been explored. Alex would have hired someone in twenty-four hours. Weeks later, Liam was still considering the decision and infuriating Alex with his apparent inaction.

In Liam's mind, decision-making can assume epic proportions. With his constant search for perfection, every decision must be the right one to avoid costly and time-consuming mistakes. He will not be pushed into what he sees as impulsive and thoughtless decisions, whether it's booking a plumber or choosing to marry.

In fairness, as Alex learnt, Liam's ability to check and recheck every detail on a purchase usually ended in the right decision. Alex learnt to take a breath, lighten up on the nagging, and understand they would end up with a good deal. Over time, it fell to Alex to make strategic decisions about investments while Liam managed the detailed decisions that made life easier at home.

In communication, their challenges, unsurprisingly, centred around Alex's directness and lack of sensitivity, and Liam's overly sensitive nature. Liam tended to make negative, closed statements such as, 'We can't afford this, can we?' He wanted Alex to give him more detail so he could make an informed decision, but Alex perceived this as negative and didn't bother pursuing it. He clocked it up as yet another negative reaction from Liam.

Meanwhile, Liam feels Alex ignores his needs. Alex doesn't notice that Liam has disappeared into a quiet zone and is walking around with pursed lips, bottling everything inside. When he's in this state, new problems seem to snowball in Liam's mind. He sees other things that are wrong, such as Alex taking him, and the work he does around the house, for granted.

Although it was understood Liam managed the house, he feels it is never appreciated. Bringing in the washing and stocking up the pantry are chores that seem to fall under Alex's radar. He doesn't notice and Liam never brings it to his attention because he feels that these things should be noticed without him saying anything. So, Liam fumes silently. On the bigger issues, he becomes so fuelled by negative feelings that it almost immobilises him. Instead of acting, he plays the issue on a mental loop, over and over, stoking the fire on his gloomy feelings.

Alex needs to understand what's important to Liam and become more aware of his nonverbal clues when he's upset and bottling things up. As they grow together, Alex has learnt to notice the effort and value Liam puts into the relationship and remembers to say thank you. He's also learnt to watch for the signals that all might not be well in Liam World. For Liam's part, he works on speaking up and telling Alex when he needs to be appreciated and tries to frame his statements more positively.

It was long after they were married and only when they had their son, Ben, that their life began to settle down. The baby stages were fun, and as their boy grew, they found their ideas of parenting were quite complementary. Both have high expectations, believed in standards, and liked to set rules and limits. Both demanded respect.

Alex doesn't respond well to emotional scenes or drama and tends to have a quick temper, which is when Liam's sensitivity kicks in. Alex was able to help Ben set big picture goals and Liam taught their son time management and how to gather information for problems and assignments. Neither parent likes to be disrespected but when it comes to conflict Alex was more adept at handling the difficult teenage years. Being more reserved, Liam often had to work at keeping close to his son. Overall, they worked well together as parents.

Life settled into an acceptable routine as Ben approached adulthood. Liam and Alex had grown somewhat apart with separate interests and friends and sex was no longer that interesting, but life was stable and secure—everything Liam has always wanted. He missed romance and craved Alex's attention, but felt okay about their life.

Then Liam met Morgan. A friend of a friend, they were doing a ceramics course together. Morgan listened. He was attentive and made Liam laugh in a way he hadn't laughed in a long time. And he pursued Liam relentlessly. Liam was flattered and surely it was harmless, after all, he was in love with Alex. But Morgan was used to getting what he wanted and before he knew what was happening, Liam found himself caught up in a tsunami of romance. It was never going to last.

Horrified, Liam was paralysed with guilt at what he had done. One of his most enduring traits is loyalty. He and Alex joked that if one of them was ever going to have an affair, it would be Alex. Mortified, he cut all contact with Morgan after a couple of weeks. But the damage was in his own head. He replayed silent scenes endlessly. Scenes of lying to Alex, of sharing an intimate meal with Morgan. He replayed every minute of his two-week affair for months. He was beside himself with worry that Alex would find out. Finally, he made the decision to tell him.

Despite his fear of conflict, Liam knew it had to be better than his internal suffering. The affair was a huge mistake, he was sorry, and he felt guilty about it. He thought that if he was honest, admit he'd had the fling, but it was now over, Alex would see it as a stupid mistake and forgive him. It wouldn't be easy, but it was a problem shared and after all, what is a relationship if you can't be honest? Liam couldn't have been more wrong. Alex hated failure. He hated weakness and he hated betrayal. He thought he was in control of his life and Liam's infidelity made a mockery of everything they had built together. His reaction was fearsome. He saw the entire marriage as a failure.

When Alex said he would leave, Liam's world disintegrated. For a week, he could barely function. But in that time, Alex realised he wouldn't be leaving. To acknowledge that his partner had cheated on him, that he hadn't been good enough to sustain their relationship, would be a humiliation and shame he would not share. He would also not give up his money in divorce. He could afford it, but the thought of losing it was intolerable.

The incident would remain private and he would remain in a tolerable, shameful, and now unhappy relationship. Liam suffered the most. Locked in a cage of guilt, Alex needed to see him suffering. And whenever Liam felt a little more confident, Alex reminded him of what he had done and took every opportunity to punish him. He had total control and therefore the relationship was unequal. As the years went by, the anger dwindled, and the relationship formed a fragile sense of team again. After all, there were many years of love and friendship between them. Alex has a devoted partner on whom he can always rely. Liam has financial security and stability. But it will never be the same.

Lime and Apple

Limes and Apples share the left-brain traits of analysis, logic, and practicality; though one is lightning-fast and the other more deliberate. Limes are comfortable with Apples' workaholic natures as it fits in with their own sense of responsibility and duty. They admire Apples' intelligence and ability to make things happen. Apples enjoy Limes' competence and ability to think things through with reason. Together they make sound decisions.

Potential Problems

Apples like the efficiency of a Lime-run household, but they have little interest in contributing and they rarely notice, so they tend to take the Lime for granted. They become easily frustrated with the Lime's desire for home and hearth rather than action. Apples are prone to rule-breaking and unconventional ways, which can create major stress for Limes.

Liam and Manuela: the Lime and the Mango

When Liam started looking for a partner, he did so with the seriousness with which he approached everything else in his life. It was typically methodical, because to choose wrongly would mean making a mistake. That would mean embarrassment, which Liam avoided at all costs. Once he had determined the criteria for his perfect partner, he registered his profile on an internet dating app. This was the perfect medium for him to vet potential lovers with maximum efficiency. After several trials, he met Manuela, who worked for a pharmaceutical company, and slowly romance blossomed. But Liam didn't trust easily. A sensitive soul, he kept a carefully built wall around his emotions, afraid to be hurt and let down.

At first, Manu took this as being super shy, but as they got to know each other, she realised this was who Liam was and accepted but did not understand his reserved style. Used to being on his guard, Liam sometimes slowed things down himself by misinterpreting signs when Manu had no hidden agenda. Because Limes are such great observers of human nature, they tend to think others are studying them with equal intensity. He resisted at first, but Manu's Mango superpower of persuasion didn't take long to work its magic and he let Manu move in. First into his head, then into his heart and finally into his home.

Liam treasured his home. Over the years, he had carefully cultivated designer pieces from all over the world. As an interior designer, Liam's sense of beauty and harmony was showcased in a seamless, tranquil environment.

When Manu first moved in, Liam was anxious. His possessions were of the utmost importance. The carefully selected pieces—the Philippe Starck, for heaven's sake! The artwork alone … Then there were his clothes—ironed, hung, and categorised by colour. What if Manu didn't show the same respect to his things? Liam's worst fears were realised. Manu adored beautiful things and certainly spent enough money on them but did not have the same level of care and concern that Liam had.

She respected Liam's desire to cherish his possessions and was proud of the home he had created but her own wardrobe was total disorder. Liam always had to keep the door closed— it almost hurt his eyes to see how she hung and stored her clothes. Still, it was a small price to pay for being with Manu.

With Manu in his life, Liam now actually spent more time in the beautiful home he had created. He'd always liked being at home alone but found he also enjoyed the predictability of a long-term relationship. He started planning their evening meals and leaving work earlier to come home and prepare them. Liam has a love for food and was keen to share his passion. Manu was equally enthusiastic about food and wine and when she wasn't eating out for work, she loved coming home to scented candles and beautifully prepared meals. It was a haven for her. Liam cooked and cleaned—what a catch!

Liam continued to look after the running of the house. He compiled a list of chores to do each day, divided into daily and weekly tasks, and expected that each chore should be highlighted in green when they were completed. The household budget, along with the wine collection, was detailed on a spreadsheet. Liam didn't have a cleaner because they didn't do it properly. He preferred to clean the house himself, to perfection.

Manu thought it was kind of sweet that Liam had this organisation thing down pat, but she simply ignored it. If she remembered—or if it was something she wanted done—she'd highlight the completed chores and then hug Liam into submission whenever he went on about his rules. And there were rules. This was a source of stress for Liam, who expected Manu to complete her assigned jobs with accuracy and competence. There was a "right" way to do everything and those of you who've ever stacked a Lime's dishwasher incorrectly will know what I mean.

In the fridge and the pantry, there is a place for everything. Knives must face a certain way in the drawer. Books are arranged in alphabetical order, categories, or Liam's preference—colour coding. But never mix the methods. Manu found all this charming, and tried to remember the rules, she really did. But too often she was off fluttering around some new idea.

Liam continued to manage the household affairs, which was fine by Manu until she realised how much insurance they were paying. Household, car, life, income protection, funeral, travel, flood, fire, health, long term care, liability insurance. Completely ridiculous. She left him to it. If he wanted to pay over the top home and contents, he could. But she kept her own health cover and only got travel insurance when she remembered. Liam couldn't understand why she didn't buy yearly travel insurance instead of paying per trip. He spent many sleepless nights every time she went away.

Manu had an active social life and an extensive group of friends, including her old university buddies—a group that had expanded as they married and settled down. They tried to get together every weekend and often went away in large groups. While Liam was confident in small groups of people he knew, he constantly felt uncomfortable in this group. He was a good listener, but even good listeners get bored and frustrated when they're not asked any questions. Liam has always been quick to like and dislike and knew from the beginning that this group wasn't for him.

All of Manu's friends worked in pharmaceuticals and they constantly talked shop, which was limiting for Liam. He felt they breached courtesy standards by sticking to topics which excluded him. After a while, Liam refused to take part in these dinners. He considered separate activities and groups of friends to be healthy for a relationship, but not when the friends make up the bulk of your partner's social circle. Manu loved her crew. They all got on so well and they just loved Liam. He was being way too sensitive. Liam was upset and stressed and refused to be subjected to dinners where he felt inadequate despite being an expert in his own field.

This led to a much-heated discussion. Neither liked arguing, but Manu would forget about it within the hour while Liam was still stewing on it days later. Manu thought he was being silly and imagining the problem; Liam felt childish but was resolute in his decision to stay away from this group of friends. He couldn't see why they had to break the rules of social interaction. He focused on what he saw as their mistakes.

In the end, there was little compromise. Both approached the problem from an emotional perspective and Manu would not give up her besties. She tried to see them a little less frequently, but it seemed every time they were doing something, it was something she couldn't bear to miss. Then she was torn, because everyone was there with their partners and she missed Liam … why was he such a bore?

Regaling her friends with funny stories of their arguments, they promised to include Liam more and, bit by bit, she edged him back in. Begrudgingly, he learned to enjoy them, even finding his own, quieter type among them.

At first, Manu thought Liam's decision-making was a joke. When they needed a plumber, he researched the existing problem first to see if he could fix it and looked at alternate ways of approaching it. He interviewed plumbers and analysed who provided the best value. She learned Liam wouldn't touch a problem until every alternative had been explored. Manu was astounded. She would have had the problem fixed in 24 hours. Instead, Liam was still considering the decision weeks later. Baffled, and a bit frustrated by his inaction, Manu moves on to other things. But decision-making can assume epic proportions in Liam's mind. In his constant search for perfection, any decision must be the right one to avoid costly and time-consuming mistakes. He will not be pushed into what he sees as impulsive and thoughtless decisions, whether it's booking a plumber or choosing to marry.

In fairness, as Manu learnt, Liam's ability to check and recheck every detail on a purchase usually ended in making better decisions. She learnt to take a breath and leave it to him, knowing they would always get a good deal. She liked to be involved in the big decisions, like parties and holidays, but was happy for Liam to manage the detail that made life easier at home.

In communication, their challenges came from their opposite perspectives. Manu had a helicopter view that gave her an overall sense of what needed to happen. Liam saw detail and was unable to have a conversation without it. Manu would throw out a problem and move on to three other topics while Liam was still figuring out the first problem. Every time Manu had an idea, Liam quashed it before she had a chance to finish explaining—a response Liam considers to be constructive and practical feedback.

But when Liam withdraws into himself, all problems seem to snowball and take on magnified proportions. Despite Manu's manic tornado of a life, she will eventually notice Liam's pain and will stop to console and help get life into perspective for him. She has also learnt that when she interrupts him, she needs to wait a minute for his brain to shift gears and reset.

Although it was understood Liam manages the house, he feels it is never appreciated. Things like bringing the washing in and stocking the pantry fall under Manu's radar. She doesn't notice and he never brings it to her attention, because he feels that these things should be noticed without him saying anything. So, he silently fumes. On the bigger issues, Liam can become so fuelled by negative feelings that it almost immobilises him. Instead of acting, he plays the issue over and over in his mind, stoking the fire of gloomy feelings.

Manu needs to understand what's important to Liam and become more aware of his nonverbal clues when he's upset and bottling things up. As they grow together, Manu has learnt to notice the effort and value Liam puts into the relationship and say thank you. She's also learnt to watch for the signals that all might not be well in Liam World. For his part, Liam works on speaking up and telling Manu when he needs to be appreciated and tries to frame his statements more positively. By the time they were married and had their son Ben, life had settled into a place of contentment and a good understanding of their differences.

Manu enjoys motherhood and doesn't let it slow her down—well, not much. Liam was an attentive and worried dad, always concerned that Ben wasn't warm enough, or was climbing too high, or had the wrong friends. Manu's parenting style was more casual, and while it was an area of bickering between them, she was quietly grateful that Liam was always there. She knew he wouldn't let anything fall through the cracks when it came to looking after Ben. Through school, Liam was the one who organised lunchboxes and playdates, took part in football committees, and ensured assignments were done on time. He was better at it. He felt Manu lacked discipline, so he oversaw that as well. She was not a bad mother, she was just, from Liam's perspective, a little loose.

Life settled into an acceptable routine, but Liam and Manu had grown somewhat apart as their careers had soared and their travel increased. Ben was almost grown up. Life was stable and secure—everything Liam had always wanted. He missed and craved romance, but that was okay.

Then Liam met Morgan. A friend of a friend, they were doing a ceramics course together. Morgan listened. She was attentive and made Liam laugh in a way he hadn't laughed in a long time. And she pursued Liam relentlessly. Liam was flattered and surely it was harmless, after all, he was in love with Manu. But Morgan was used to getting what she wanted and before he knew what was happening, Liam found himself caught up in a tsunami of romance. It was never going to last.

Horrified, Liam was paralysed with guilt at what he had done. One of his most enduring traits was loyalty. He and Manu joked that if one of them was ever going to have an affair, it would be Manu. Mortified, Liam cut all contact with Morgan after a couple of weeks. But the damage was in his own head. He replayed silent scenes over and over. Scenes of lying to Manu, of sharing an intimate meal with Morgan. He replayed every minute of his two-week affair and was beside himself with worry that Manu would find out. Finally, he made the decision to tell her.

Despite his fear of conflict, Liam knew it had to be better than his internal suffering. The affair was a huge mistake, he was sorry, and he felt guilty about it. He thought that if he was honest, admit he'd had the fling but was now over, Manu would see it as a stupid mistake and forgive him. It wouldn't be easy, but it was a problem shared and after all, what is a relationship if you can't be honest?

Manu was devastated. Not her beautiful, solid, loyal Liam? This had to be a mistake! More than anything, she was shocked and hurt. How could anybody cheat on her? But in a short time, the irony dawned. Damn it, it should have been her that had the affair! That's what they'd always said. It was almost funny. And there was poor old Liam, suffering more than she ever would. He loved her; she knew it. She loved him. But maybe they just hadn't been paying enough attention to each other of late. Why else would he get caught up with someone else? She was hurt, there was no doubt, but she could also see the funny and realistic side. They would work this out, like they worked through everything.

It took a little time, but Liam adores his crazy, fun-loving Manu who reminds him not to take life so seriously. And Manu loves Liam for the beautiful home he's created, a place of calm and order, a place to come home and recharge.

Lime and Mango

Mangoes provide Limes with the carefree child to be taken care of, while delighting them with the chance to see the world differently. Limes love that Mangoes have the social skills to take the heat in demanding situations and let Limes choose who they want to socialise with. Mangoes love the Limes' elegant ability to handle any crisis with dignity, and for providing a place of safe harbour away from melodrama where they can rest and be loved.

Potential Problems

While these opposites have many opportunities for conflict, the most common is Limes' reluctance to spend money and Mangoes' tendency to spend more than they earn. Mangoes can see their Lime partners as the Fun Police, but Limes will argue they *do* have fun—it's just that to enjoy the fun, they have to know they can afford it.

Liam and Brooklyn: the Lime and the Banana

When Liam started looking for a partner, he did so with the seriousness with which he approached everything else in his life. It was typically methodical, because to choose wrongly would mean making a mistake. That would mean embarrassment, which Liam avoided at all costs. Once he'd determined the criteria for his perfect partner, he registered his profile on an internet dating service app—the perfect medium for him to vet potential lovers with maximum efficiency. After several trials, he met Brooklyn, who worked for a pharmaceutical company, and slowly romance blossomed. But Liam didn't trust easily. A sensitive soul, he kept a carefully built wall around his emotions, afraid to be hurt and let down.

At first, Brooklyn took this as extreme shyness, but as they got to know each other, she realised this was who Liam was and accepted his reserved style. She wasn't much of a show pony herself. Liam was used to being on his guard and sometimes slowed things down by misinterpreting signs when the transparent Brooklyn had no hidden agenda. Limes are great observers of human nature and tend to think others are studying them with equal intensity. Neither was in any rush so when Brooklyn eventually moved in with Liam, they both felt ready.

Liam treasured his home. Over the years, he'd carefully cultivated designer pieces from all over the world. As an interior designer, Liam's sense of beauty and harmony was showcased in a seamless, tranquil environment. He was a little nervous. His possessions were of the utmost importance. The carefully selected pieces—the Philippe Starck, for heaven's sake! The artwork! Then there were his clothes, ironed, hung and categorised by colour. Maybe Brooklyn wouldn't show the same respect he did?

He needn't have worried about his expensive artwork. Brooklyn had little knowledge of art but enjoyed learning from Liam and looking after the things he valued. Clothes were a different story—they really weren't that important to her. Over time, she left Liam to organise her side of the wardrobe even though she never bought into the colour coding.

With Brooklyn in his life, Liam now actually spent more time in the beautiful home he had created. He'd always liked being at home alone but found he also enjoyed the predictability of a long-term relationship. He started planning their evening meals and leaving work earlier to come home and prepare them. Liam had a love of food and was keen to share his passion. Brooklyn was thrilled to find someone to cook for her. She also enjoyed cooking so between them they took turns to cook and clean.

Liam continued to look after the running of the house. He compiled a list of chores to do each day, divided into daily and weekly tasks, and expected that each chore should be highlighted in green highlighter when they were completed. The household budget, along with the wine collection, was detailed on a spreadsheet. Liam didn't have a cleaner because they didn't do it properly; he preferred to clean the house himself, to perfection.

Brooklyn privately thought this was way over the top. She did her best to complete the tasks and although it wasn't always up to scratch, Liam found it hard to be critical. She did so much around the house and was always watching out for him. In some ways, she was too nice. But there were plenty of rules. There was a "right" way to do everything, and anyone who has ever stacked a Lime's dishwasher incorrectly will know what I mean.

In the fridge and the pantry, there is a place for everything. Knives must face a certain way in the drawer. Books must be arranged in alphabetical order, categories, or Liam's preference—colour coding. But never mix the methods. Brooklyn found all this charming and funny, and loved the organisation that Liam bought into his home. She tried to remember the rules, she really did. And when she didn't, she made sure to make up for it with romantic touches like love notes and cooking Liam's favourite treats.

It was understood Liam managed the house, but Brooklyn made an equal contribution. Together they organised everything from grocery shopping to housework. The one bone of contention Liam had was that Brooklyn didn't take the same level of care. She didn't mind if people popped in and the breakfast dishes were in the sink or the beds unmade. To Liam, this was not negotiable. Everything had to be clean and tidy before he left for work. He is enormously frustrated with Brooklyn's casual attitude, even more so when she laughs it off. He knows it's not a reason for divorce, but he feels resentful that Brooklyn doesn't take tidiness seriously.

Liam continued to manage the household affairs, which was okay, but Brooklyn had never met anyone with so much insurance. Household, car, life, income protection, funeral, travel, flood, fire, health, long term care, liability insurance. Weird, if you think about it. She tried to talk him out of it as she could see how much it was costing them, but he would not be swayed. In order to sleep at night, he needed that insurance.

Brooklyn loved people and had a wide group of friends, including her old university buddies—a group that had expanded as they married and settled down. They tried to get together every weekend and often went away in large groups. While Liam was confident in small groups of people he knew, he constantly felt uncomfortable in this group. He was a good listener, but even good listeners get bored and frustrated when they're not asked any questions. Liam has always been quick to like and dislike and knew from the beginning that this group wasn't for him.

All of Brooklyn's friends worked in pharmaceuticals and they constantly talked shop, which was limiting for Liam. He felt they breached courtesy standards by sticking to topics which excluded him. After a while, Liam refused to take part in these dinners. He considered separate activities and groups of friends to be healthy for a relationship, but not when the friends make up the bulk of your partner's social circle. Brooklyn loved her crew. They all got on so well and they just loved Liam! He was being way too sensitive. Liam was upset and stressed and refused to be subjected to dinners where he felt inadequate despite being an expert in his own field.

But they didn't talk about it much. Brooklyn was distressed that her soulmate didn't like her best friends. She hated arguing about it and thought if she left Liam alone for a bit he would come around. Liam was petulant when Brooklyn went out alone and she was wracked with guilt. Because neither liked to address the problem, it went unresolved before slowly morphing into some sort of compromise. When Liam went away for work, Brooklyn took the opportunity to see her friends, which left more time for him. She bargained with Liam to come out with them occasionally and pleaded with her friends to give him a chance. Begrudgingly, he learned to enjoy their company, even finding his own, quieter type amongst them.

Brooklyn discovered that Liam took his own time to make decisions. When a plumber was needed, he researched the existing problem to see if he could fix it and looked at alternate ways of addressing it. He interviewed plumbers and analysed who provided the best value. He wouldn't touch a problem until every alternative had been explored. Brooklyn admired this approach because she knew she would be more slapdash about it. If he did everything this way it was less work for her, and they would never make a bad decision!

Decision-making can assume epic proportions in Liam's mind. In his constant search for perfection, any decision must be the right one to avoid costly and time-consuming mistakes. He will not be pushed into what he sees as impulsive and thoughtless decisions, whether it's booking a plumber or choosing to marry.

In many ways, Liam and Brooklyn's relationship was stable and solid. They rarely had problems communicating. Neither rushed the other, nor invaded their space. There was a respect for each other's opinion. Brooklyn appreciated Liam's attentiveness and desire for perfection and tried desperately not to finish his sentences for him. Liam recognised and loved how much effort Brooklyn put into their relationship. It wasn't always perfect, but compared to many of their volatile friends, it was just fine.

Sometimes Liam withdrew into himself and his natural propensity to worry caused his problems to loom larger than they were. At first, Brooklyn had mixed success with her efforts to help by offering solutions or encouraging him to talk. Over time, she learnt that it was okay to leave Liam in his own headspace until he was ready to open up.

Both Liam and Brooklyn had a strong sense of family and there was no doubt that they wanted children. By the time they were married and had their son Ben, life had settled into a comfortable routine. They were content with each other and had a solid understanding of their differences. Both were devoted parents, but Brooklyn was completely besotted. They made Ben the centre of their world.

Liam was an attentive and worried dad, always concerned that Ben wasn't warm enough, or was climbing too high, or had the wrong friends. He created timelines and calendars for all Ben's activities to help Brooklyn remember them all. He taught Ben to be curious and to question the world around him.

Brooklyn was patient and kind—the ultimate nurturing mum. Nothing seemed to phase her and that really got on Liam's nerves. But between them, they managed to iron out any minor disagreements and Brooklyn was grateful for Liam's insistent worry and efficiency. She knew he wouldn't let anything fall through the cracks when it came to looking after Ben.

Liam and Brooklyn had grown together with very few major arguments. They both travelled for work, and if they were honest, that was often the most exciting part of their lives. Ben was almost grown up and they were stable and secure, everything Liam had always wanted—just a little boring. Was this all there was?

Around this time, Liam met Morgan. A friend of a friend, they were doing a ceramics course together. Morgan listened. She was attentive. She made Liam laugh in a way he hadn't laughed for a long time. And she pursued Liam relentlessly. Liam was flattered and surely it was harmless. After all, he was in love with Brooklyn. But Morgan was used to getting what she wanted and before he knew what was happening, Liam found himself caught up in a tsunami of romance. It was never going to last.

Liam was horrified and paralysed with guilt at what he had done. One of his most enduring traits was loyalty. He and Brooklyn always used to joke that he was too loyal to have an affair and she was too lazy. And now it was him! How could it be? Mortified, he cut all contact with Morgan after a couple of weeks. But the damage was in his own head. He replayed silent scenes over and over. Scenes of lying to Brooklyn, of sharing an intimate meal with Morgan. For months, he replayed every minute of their two-week affair. He was beside himself with worry that Brooklyn would find out. Finally, he made the decision to tell her.

Despite his fear of conflict, he knew it had to be better than this suffering. The affair was a huge mistake, he was sorry, and he felt guilty about it. He thought if he was honest, admit he'd had the fling, but it was now over, Brooklyn would see it as a stupid mistake and forgive him. It wouldn't be easy, but it was a problem shared and, after all, what is a relationship if you can't be honest?

Brooklyn was devastated. Not her beautiful, solid, loyal Liam? This had to be a mistake! She was hurt to the core. She cried for days on end, spent hours on the phone to her mother and her girlfriends, crying and talking. Was it her fault? She had let herself go, she was fat, and old! Maybe she wasn't looking after herself as well as she used to and now … she had lost him. But … how could he?

She simply could not imagine herself without the family life they had created. If she left the marriage, there would never be anyone like Liam to love her again. She would never find anyone else and she'd be alone forever. Liam loved her. She knew he did. And he was so sorry. He must feel so dreadful, barely able to sleep. It was eating him up, she could see. He was suffering just as much as she was. She was in pain, but so was he. And if anyone could make a relationship work, she could.

Together, they rebuilt their lives. For a long time they suffered in their own ways, but they emerged stronger than before. Liam and Brooklyn had faced and survived their only major test. He adores the warmth and harmony she brings to their home, and she loves the loyal man who will never stray again.

Lime and Banana

Limes and Bananas share a common pace of speech and thinking, as well as a desire to do the right thing. They both love a peaceful, harmonious life. Limes enjoy Bananas' kindness, thoughtfulness, and patience, and that they never push them into anything. Bananas enjoy that they don't need to worry about paying bills or booking meetings at the school when their efficient Lime is around.

Potential Problems

Challenges arise when the pragmatic Lime simply can't understand the Banana's idealism, wanting to save everything from the global environment to an injured bird. They become frustrated with their Banana's need to be away helping others, instead of building a safe home for them both.

Bananas demand a depth of romance and loving that the Lime finds difficult to comprehend and is often confused about how to provide. The Lime wants to do the right thing but prefers more realistic displays of affection, like ensuring the Banana's fair share of the bills gets paid each month. Bananas and Limes are not quick decision-makers and may become paralysed by indecision. This can pose a problem when a fast decision is needed, and both need more time to consider.

Liam and Lana: the Double Lime

When Liam was looking for a partner, he did so with the seriousness with which he approached everything else in his life. It was typically methodical because to choose wrongly would mean making a mistake. That would mean embarrassment, which Liam avoided at all costs. Once he had determined the criteria for the perfect partner, he registered his profile on an internet dating site—the perfect medium for him to vet potential lovers with maximum efficiency. After several trials, he met Lana, who worked for a pharmaceutical company, and slowly romance blossomed. But Liam didn't trust easily. A sensitive soul, he kept a carefully built wall around his emotions, afraid to be hurt and let down.

As it turned out, Lana didn't trust easily either. She was nervous about meeting someone on a dating site but felt it was the most efficient way to match likes. She recognised a kindred spirit in Liam. They were both reserved and anxious about making the wrong decision, so at first, they circled around each other a little warily. They watched and listened; listened and watched. And in surprisingly little time by their standards, they had made the decision to move in together.

Liam treasured his home. Over the years, he'd carefully cultivated designer pieces from all over the world. As an interior designer, Liam's sense of beauty and harmony was showcased in a seamless, tranquil environment. His possessions were of the utmost importance. The carefully selected pieces. The artwork. Then there were his clothes, ironed, hung, and categorised by colour. Somehow, he just knew that Lana would respect this. She didn't have the same design finesse or knowledge of art, but she was grateful to have the opportunity to enjoy these beautiful pieces. She didn't fold her underwear and rotate them for equal use, but she did colour-code her wardrobe and she did like to file her books by colour. Liam was ecstatic. Just the way he liked it!

With Lana in his life, Liam now spent more time in the beautiful home he had created. He had always liked being at home alone but found he also enjoyed the predictability of a long-term relationship. He started planning their evening meals and leaving work earlier to come home and prepare them. Liam had a love of food and was keen to share his passion. Lana was thrilled to find someone to cook for her. She was quite particular about her food. She was lactose intolerant and wasn't keen on trying new things. She ate fish but not shellfish and preferred to only eat certain types of nuts. She needed to eat at a specific time to manage her potential hypoglycaemia.

Liam loved to shop, prepare, and cook their meals and he took the time to do it properly. But after a while he knew Lana was not fully appreciating his effort or sharing his joy of eating the meals. She was relieved when he bought it up. Not wanting to offend Liam, she had tried to eat his creations but could not muster up the enthusiasm. She also loved to cook, but only the meals she liked. They decided to prepare and cook their own dinners, together, and sit down to eat at the same time, only eat different things. Each was responsible for cleaning up their own mess. It was fair and reasonable.

Liam's home was special to him, so he continued to look after the running of the house. He compiled a list of chores to do each day, divided into daily and weekly tasks and expected each chore should be highlighted in green when they were completed. The household budget, along with the wine collection, was detailed on a spreadsheet. He didn't have a cleaner because they didn't do it properly. He preferred to clean his own house to perfection. Imagine his delight when he found that Lana wanted to help with the cleaning. They cleaned daily which left their weekends free. Lana didn't mind using a highlighter but soon introduced a more sophisticated tool to manage their shared projects. Her way was more efficient, and there was no paper waste. They agreed on the rules. There was a "right" way to do everything and anyone who's ever stacked a Lime's dishwasher incorrectly will know what I mean. In the fridge and the pantry there is a place for everything. Knives must face a certain way in the drawer, and storage … well that was a joy in itself!

With Lana's approval, Liam continued to manage the household affairs. He was the only person she had met who had more insurance than her. Household, car, life, income protection, funeral, travel, flood, fire, health, long term care, liability insurance. It really was a bit over the top, but when you thought about it, all essential. Like Liam, Lana had a select group of friends, including her old university buddies, a group that had started small but expanded as they got married and settled down. They tried to get together pretty much every weekend, and often went away in large groups.

While Liam was confident in small groups of people he knew, he constantly felt uncomfortable in this group. He was a good listener, but even good listeners get bored and frustrated when they're not asked any questions. Liam has always been quick to like and dislike and knew from the beginning that this group wasn't for him.

All of the friends worked in pharmaceuticals and talked shop, which was limiting for Liam. He felt they breached courtesy standards by sticking to topics which excluded him. After a while, Liam refused to take part in these dinners. He was upset and stressed and refused to be subjected to situations where he felt inadequate despite being an expert in his own field. He considered separate activities and groups of friends to be healthy for a relationship, but not when the friends make up the bulk of your partner's social circle.

Lana was upset that Liam was so adamant in refusing to take part and upset with her friends for not making more of an effort. Lana enjoyed her friends, but the group had become too big. These days, she preferred to be with one or two of them at a time. After examining the problem from all angles and worrying for too many nights than she cared to admit, she decided to start seeing her favourites separately away from the large group. Sometimes Liam came with her, which worked out well, but she knew they would always be her special friends. She ended up backing away from the large group altogether.

Lana had never come across anyone who went out about decision-making the way she did. With previous partners she was frustrated with their carefree purchases, their throwaway decisions, and their lack of thought. Liam gave adequate thought to each decision he made. When they needed a plumber, he researched the existing problem to see if he could fix it and looked at alternate ways to address it. He interviewed plumbers and analysed who provided the best value. He wouldn't touch a problem until every alternative had been explored, and Lana was happy with this approach. If they did everything Liam's way, they'd never make a bad decision!

Decision-making can assume epic proportions in Liam's mind. In his constant search for perfection, any decision must be the right one to avoid costly and time-consuming mistakes. He would not be pushed into what he sees as impulsive and thoughtless decisions, whether it's booking a plumber or choosing to marry. This makes complete sense to Lana.

A relationship between two Limes can be stable and problem free. There is little to argue beyond whether to make the caramelised apple pudding or the frangipane tart for dinner guests. Liam and Lana are content with quiet time alone, and nighttime at their house is music and low lighting, with the occasional binge series on TV. Their conversation is thoughtful, both are good listeners, and neither speaks unnecessarily, although Lana tends to offer too much detail about problems she encounters at work.

They have quiet dinners with select and loyal friends. They did yoga together and meditated. Liam painted and drew, and Lana played piano. If one of them withdrew into themselves through a natural propensity to worry, the other one worried with them, hovering until the moment passed. The tension came when the worry manifested itself into a huge ball of stress. If one had become wound up and was holding their stress inside, it would eventually come out in a burst, but even then, Liam and Lana eventually saw and understood what was happening. They had a balanced, equal, and mostly calm relationship.

By the time they were married and had their son Ben, life had settled into a place of contentment and a genuine understanding of their differences. Both had a strong sense of responsibility and of family loyalty. They approached parenthood with the same precision they did anything which was brilliant for organising playdates and meals and as Ben got older, assignments. But parenting created stress and Liam and Lana soon had their first major argument. The baby would not feed when Lana wanted. He did not sleep the way Lana planned. He cried a lot. Liam and Lana would plan a quiet meal together and Ben would wake up and cry the moment they sat down to eat. Lana was exhausted. Liam couldn't see why Lana couldn't manage the baby with the same system they had always used. Lana wasn't trying hard enough and needed her mother around to help. This annoyed Liam and he felt like a failure. But they got through it. They survived and emerged from the parenting tunnel with their relationship intact.

Liam was an attentive and worried dad, always concerned that Ben wasn't warm enough, or was climbing too high, or had the wrong friends. He created timelines and calendars for all Ben's activities and taught Ben to question the world. Liam and Lana went to parent-teacher meetings together and dutifully noted everything Ben needed help with.

Life had settled into a comfortable routine. Liam and Lana both travelled for work, and if they were honest, that was often the most exciting part of their lives. Lana's travel took her away from home for weeks at a time.

Ben was almost grown up and their lives were stable and secure, everything Liam had always wanted—just a little boring. Was this all there was?

Around this time Liam met Morgan. A friend of a friend, they were doing a ceramics course together. Morgan listened. She was attentive. She made Liam laugh in a way he hadn't laughed for a long time. And she pursued Liam relentlessly. He was flattered and surely it was harmless. After all, he was in love with Lana. But Morgan was used to getting what she wanted and before he knew what was happening, Liam found himself caught up in a tsunami of romance. It was never going to last.

Liam was horrified by his behaviour and paralysed with guilt. One of his most enduring traits was loyalty. He and Lana always used to joke that neither of them would ever have an affair because they were too risk averse. He had taken that risk and now he was paying the price. How could he have done this? Mortified, he cut all contact with Morgan after a couple of weeks. But the damage was in his own head. He replayed silent scenes over and over. Scenes of lying to Lana, of sharing an intimate meal with Morgan. For months, he replayed every minute of their two-week affair. He was beside himself with worry that Lana would find out. Finally, he made the decision to tell her.

Despite his fear of conflict, he knew it had to be better than this suffering. The affair was a huge mistake. He was sorry, and he felt guilty about it. He thought that if he was honest, admit he'd had the fling, but it was now over, Lana would see it as a stupid mistake and forgive him. It wouldn't be easy, but it was a problem shared and after all, what is a relationship if you can't be honest? He wasn't sure how it would end, but he knew he couldn't keep it inside. Lana's world was shattered. She would never forgive him. She moved him into the spare bedroom while she thought through all her alternatives, but after many weeks, it always returned to one thought. This house was as much hers now as it was Liam's. She had invested so much care and effort and money into it and she would not give it up. It was the last solid thing they had.

As much as she hated Liam for what he had done, they couldn't afford a divorce. The idea of splitting all their carefully acquired assets and starting again was unthinkable. No, she would stay. But she would never, ever, forgive. Liam and Lana began to live separate and very unhappy lives.

Two Limes together

When they are happily ensconced in domestic bliss, Limes love to be the devoted partner. They take great pleasure in contributing to a happy and stable family life and will gladly assume the role set for them. Two Limes together often have a domestic life many envy. They set up home and develop a community around them through school and children's activities. Before long, they will have a steady group of local friends with whom they share common activities and regular routines, such as children's sport on the weekends or a regular restaurant on Saturday night. Together, Limes have familiarity and predictability, which in turn gives them the peace and harmony they seek.

Potential Problems

Limes can become overly critical. If both are in a nitpicky mood and believe their way is the best way to run a house, there can be a lot of angst. Both are prone to high levels of stress, and at times neither one can support the other. Each will have their own idea of perfection and need to be mindful of overloading each other with specifics. The best way forward is to stop and check the facts for accuracy before moving on.

And never have an affair. Just saying.

How to Handle the Lime in your life

If you're interested in a Lime who is new on the scene, don't hesitate to pursue them. They may be mutually interested but will be too busy weighing up the pros and cons of calling you to actually call. They may take things slowly, but the rewards of a rich relationship are worth it. Try not to mistake reserve for indifference. Your Lime is extremely sensitive and cares deeply; they just don't see the need to wear their hearts on their sleeve.

Change, no matter how small, is unsettling for a Lime. Redecorating a room or adding a timber deck can be stressful, so imagine what moving to a new house can do to them. Be patient with your Lime partner. Introduce new ideas gradually to give them time to digest the change. Initial bursts of excitement may be met with horror, which can be misconstrued as negativity.

In fact, the Lime's default setting is initially to question, which can be interpreted as a negative response, and they can be particularly abrasive to unplanned ideas. You may have also unwittingly interrupted the Lime's schedule. They may appear to be sitting and not doing anything, but that doesn't mean the introspective Lime isn't busy inside their head. Give them time to chew on the idea for a while and you might find your Lime more amenable to your original thought. For best results, introduce your idea gently, then leave it to marinate. When you have an issue to discuss, give your Lime a heads-up so they can prepare their thoughts beforehand. Limes do their best thinking when they're left alone to reflect.

Don't force a Lime into doing what you want to do because you're convinced it's a terrific idea. If they don't want to go skiing, keep this activity for yourself. It's possible the reluctance has nothing to do with you: they simply don't want to ski. Stay flexible, even if your Lime partner can't be. Try to find compromises around their rules. Help them to live in the present—they can't save everything for a rainy day.

Take the lead with friends and when accepting invitations to soften any pressure your Lime may feel in social situations. Introduce them to like-minded others and don't leave them if you feel there may be genuine tension. If they're not as witty or fabulous as you expected with strangers, so what? It's no reflection on you. If it's about your ego, you may want to rethink the relationship. When Limes launch into a detailed story, stop and listen. Everyone deserves the courtesy of being listened to.

Don't tease them incessantly. Limes genuinely dislike being teased and you may trigger a more serious confrontation. Don't treat jealousy flippantly. They would never raise an emotion like this lightly, so if it's on the table, it means they're serious. Acknowledge their fears and provide reassurance. When you confront Limes about their behaviour, expect their first reaction to be defensive. It's the Lime's nature to sound right but is often just a gut reaction. Try expressing your feelings without blame, then let them process at their own pace. You may need to come back to it a couple of times. Limes need time to think and to force them into a response is unproductive. Limes have long memories and don't forgive easily. Make sure then that you can forgive them, and importantly be ready to forgive yourself.

Appreciate the security Limes bring and the home base they provide and tell them. Limes are remarkably consistent compared to the rest of us, which stems beautifully from having a regular routine, using the same brands, and keeping the same rules. This means they are reliable, dependable, emotionally steady, and will always be there for you. To make the most of your relationship with a Lime, respect their need for space and time. Think before you speak and, if you want something, have a logical argument behind the big plan. Then life will be easier for both of you.

Tips for Limes

Expect others to be irritated by your overly detailed questions, plans, or information, and the pace at which you deliver it. When you have a lot of information to share, learn to present it in bullet points. Think about what is relevant to your partner and what's not. Avoid introducing so many details that neither you or your partner can see the big picture.

In a discussion, make sure you bring the conversations in your head out in the open. Your partner is not a mind reader and long silences without explanation don't help anyone. If you are living with a lot of noise or at an unsettlingly fast pace, ask for quiet time where you can be on your own to regroup. Don't let others be space invaders. Take control.

Work on not worrying what people other than your partner think of you. The reality is that you're not the centre of anyone else's universe and they're probably not giving you the headspace you think they are. Focus instead on the relationships that really count. To recognise the pressure you put on yourself, keep track of all the times in a week you say, 'I should'.

When you decide to take on a task, resist the urge to do more or do it better. Just do it, without putting the extra pressure on yourself. Resist the urge to find fault with imperfection and ask yourself, 'How important is this?' Accept your flaws. The right partner will love you for who you are. You should, too.

When your brain threatens to burst through worry, decision-making, or over analysis, have a game plan for coping. Choose something that works for you—listening to music, meditating, a favourite exercise. But don't try to push through it; it will only snowball. If you find yourself creating negative reasons for your new partner's behaviour, stop and reverse your thinking to fashion positive scenarios.

For example: *Why aren't they answering my texts? Don't they care anymore? Are they having drinks with someone else? Am I coming on too strong?*

Shift to: *I guess they're not answering my texts because they're busy on the phone with their mother, or they are at a gym class, or in the shower.*

When your partner creates a new challenge for you, fight the longing to say no straight away. Accept some challenges and take baby steps towards something new. You don't have to be able to speak Spanish fluently in a year. After you've had an argument, think about what you did to contribute to it. Give yourself some points for honesty and file the information for when a similar situation comes up.

Short and Sweet

Limes in a relationship

- stylish
- creative
- good housekeepers
- perfectionists
- home bodies
- don't like surprises
- hoarders
- great at managing a household budget
- ruled by too much guilt
- bring a great sensitivity and loyalty.

Lime sticking points

- don't trust easily
- feel socially inadequate
- quick to dislike people
- decision-making process frustrates some
- overanalyse
- tend to initially see things pessimistically
- overly sensitive
- don't speak up but expect accomplishments to be noticed.

Mixed Fruit

<u>Lime-Mango:</u> Limes love Mangoes' social skills and Mangoes love the safety Limes provide. Limes are frustrated by Mangoes' spending, and Mangoes hate being monitored.

<u>Lime-Banana:</u> Both share a common pace. Limes love Bananas' thoughtfulness and patience, and Bananas love Limes' efficiency. Limes get frustrated with Bananas' need to save the world, and Bananas with Limes' lack of romance.

<u>Lime-Apple:</u> Both are pragmatic. Limes like Apples' sense of duty and follow-through; Apples like Limes' competence and reason. Limes are frustrated by Apples' disregard for rules, and Apples by Limes' homebody ways.

<u>Double Limes:</u> Great home life and a predictable and harmonious existence. Two Limes together can suffer high levels of stress and worry and both can be overly critical.

Handling a Lime

- be flexible
- reserved doesn't mean indifferent
- don't force them into things you like to do
- introduce new ideas gently
- give them time to adjust to new ideas
- respect their need for space and time
- take the lead socially
- listen to their stories
- don't tease
- tell them how much you appreciate them
- take their problems seriously

- be prepared to forgive yourself in case they don't forgive you
- help them to live in the present
- treasure their loyalty
- watch for signs of worry and anxiety
- if you want variety in sex, you'll have to initiate it yourself
- don't expect compliments—your Lime is bursting with pride on the inside
- appreciate the security and stability they bring you.

Tips for Limes

- present detailed information in bullet points
- think out loud
- don't let others invade your space
- reduce the amount of "I should" in your life
- resist the urge for perfection *all* the time
- have a game plan to deal with your stress
- take baby steps when faced with new challenges
- accept your flaws
- reflect on how you might contribute to arguments.

Chapter 10

Bliss with Bananas

The sweet Fruit. Everyone needs a little Banana love in their lives. If you have a Banana partner, you should know they have devoted their lives to making yours better. They think about your needs, they listen to you, they mother you when you are sick. When you can't make it to Mitch and Alyssa's Christmas party, they bundle up a little food pack to bring home to you. You get their attention in bucket loads, and if you feel good, they feel good. Their warmth, sensitivity, and ability to connect make them appealing partners.

The Banana home is a warm place where everyone is welcome. It's filled with photos, flowers, and memories of good times. And they're a pretty laid back piece of Fruit. If you've ever found yourself going to extremes to get your partner to do something, you're probably with a Banana.

A woman once told me she tried dancing naked in heels and an apron just to get her Banana husband's attention as he watched TV—unsuccessfully. They may be devoted, but once in relaxation mode, they don't feel compelled to do anything. Apart from being natural procrastinators, they have low energy levels and crave peace and quiet.

Bananas love to talk. Their focus will be on people; real or otherwise, including dreams, movies, and books where characters have moved them. You'll often hear a Banana bemoaning how much they miss the characters when a good book or TV series finishes.

Bananas love romance and the idea of love itself. They choose from the heart. They feel it. As in most things they do, they're idealistic when choosing a mate and never stop to think it may not last forever. They demand a soul mate, a life partner. When they're in love, Bananas devote all their time to pleasing and loving the other person, which for some can become quite claustrophobic. They're generous with emotions and declaring their love for you. They need love and reassurance, that's all.

The end of a relationship is always painful, but for a Banana it is like a slow tortuous death. It's hard for Bananas to be alone. They need to be needed, to serve, and typically find someone else to love as soon as their wounds heal. Bananas place their lovers on a pedestal, which is a bummer, because there is only one way down. In the early stages of the relationship, there will be gifts and love notes, as the Banana steadfastly ignores any flaws you may have. Be careful! You are being set up to let them down.

The Banana will be putting far more into the relationship than you are. That's why it can work. They make more sacrifices to keep a relationship afloat, and they don't keep score. They're often the ones who've given up a promising career to support your dream and are genuinely happy for you. The danger for them is ending up with an overly controlling partner who doesn't give them the respect they deserve. Keep in mind that being aggressive or overly critical will result in your Banana partner feeling self-doubt and self-blame; neither of which are constructive. With careful feedback, though, your Banana partner will work hard on trying to correct themselves. It's one of their great qualities.

A Banana will tease you and insist to others that you get your own way all the time, but in truth they've often anticipated your needs and take great pleasure in meeting them. It's cold rainy weather and you've had a long day—how nice is it to come home to a rich, fragrant curry and a bottle of red breathing on the counter? Bananas are always supportive and will be sensitive to your moods and feelings. They'll typically listen to your problems with a sympathetic ear, rarely stopping to point out your mistakes like other Fruit may do.

Their natural ability to empathise allows them to put themselves in another's mental state. This means they will really feel for you, but it also means they'll feel for strangers.

I was once told the somewhat incredible story of a woman who was at a casino, saw a homeless man, and invited him back to her hotel room for the evening. She told me she felt he wasn't harmful, just tired and hungry. She asked for reassurance he wouldn't hurt her and she believed him. He slept in the bed and she slept in a chair. Imagine her husband's reaction when she told him what she had done.

Bananas' self-esteem is greatest when they see them-selves as empathic. **Being in a caring role for those closest to them gives them their sense of purpose.** They need other people to rely on them to give their own life meaning.

Often, they've grown up in a house where Mum and Dad have catered to the most demanding child. Many people have shared stories of how they gave in to an Apple sibling again and again, just so peace and harmony would be restored. As a result, the Banana has learnt not to cause a scene. When they say they don't care, they often do and are only creating a safety net for themselves.

Bananas are emotionally sensitive and cannot bear to see others suffer. They have an almost magical ability to feel other people's pain. It is empathy, their secret superpower. It's not unimaginable for them to cry at a news story. No other Fruit can put themselves in someone's place more accurately, imagining what that person is thinking and feeling.

This includes their children, which makes Banana parents a bit of a pushover. They discipline their kids, but then get upset because the kid's suffering. The kids who get to stay home from school usually have Banana parents, because secretly, there's nothing nicer for a Banana than to spend time alone with a loved one.

In their genuine desire to please their partners, Bananas can suffer. Although they don't see it that way. They will stand so others can sit. They'll take the seat without the view in the restaurant. They'll go without to give you the best cut of meat or last glass of wine in the bottle, and many Bananas have been known to lose feeling in an arm or leg holding an awkward position during sex, as long as their partner is enjoying themselves.

Bananas focus on themselves so little and on their loved ones so much that when you ask them how they are, they'll often respond with how their family is. Then they'll move quickly to ask you how *you* are, to deflect focus from themselves. By taking on their own issues and those of the people around them, Bananas tend to get overloaded.

I remember one Banana telling me she was always so busy and felt exhausted, but it turned out she was busy with other people's stuff. She'd stay all night with a friend who had a migraine or offer her spare room to a friend who had troubles at home. These are admirable qualities, but the Banana's challenge is to save time for their own wellbeing. In their zeal to care, they tend to over personalise situations that don't directly concern them.

Likewise, Bananas can get overloaded at work. They feel work needs them, can't get by without them, and they get caught up in the problems of their colleagues. This has a flow-on effect at home because they're either mentally or physically not there.

Bananas are the masters of guilt. They don't like asking for help because they feel guilty that they're wasting that person's valuable time. They feel guilty if they can't find a solution in a disagreement because they see it as their responsibility to be peacemakers. When something goes wrong, their first assumption is that it must be through some fault of their own.

As the caring, kind, patient friend and partner who does thoughtful deeds, Bananas assume others will want to do the same in return. If this doesn't happen, they can feel betrayed, and when pushed to the limit, they become staunchly unforgiving.

The stay-at-home Banana faces challenges on several fronts. Running the home and looking after their family is incredibly rewarding as they help nurture their children and watch them grow. On the other hand, being out of the paid workforce can affect their self-esteem. This, coupled with their natural guilt and eagerness to please, can lead to Bananas feeling insignificant.

Bananas often lack ego and with that can come a lack of self-worth and a belief their needs are less important than others'. The Banana's partner must be sensitive to this and dig deeper to find out what's really important to them. As they develop their confidence, strengthened by their partner's love, they can become quietly strong. The lack of ego also means Bananas are delightful company and a pleasure to be around. These are the qualities that make for a joyful relationship.

A Banana story in four different flavours

This is the story of Billie, whose first behavioural preference is extreme Banana. And here's the story of what could happen depending on which Fruit she pairs with.

Billie and Arun: the Banana and the Apple

School teacher Billie had a run of bad boyfriends. They were too lazy, too needy, too controlling. She couldn't seem to get it right. Then she met Arun, who worked in government, and there was an immediate attraction. He was handsome, strong, and confident. He made decisions about everything, so she didn't have to think at all.

Billie has a seven-year-old son. This had never been on Arun's radar. In his mind he would create a family of his own, not take in someone else's offspring. The kid already had a father, he didn't need another one. To be honest, Arun wanted Billie, not the kid, who was a pain in the proverbial. But Arun had fallen hard for Billie, and Brandon came with the package. How hard could it be?

Billie gave out her love to Arun in bucket loads. It was the most natural thing in the world for her to hug regularly and say, 'I love you.' Occasions such as birthdays gave her the opportunity to spoil him with champagne and treats. To Arun, Billie seemed almost psychic, anticipating his needs before he realised them. Just the way he liked it. Billie's friends often told Arun he should do more for her, but as he explained, Billie loved looking after him.

For the first few months, they were living in different cities, and Billie did all she could to stay in touch. She sent Arun flowers. Ten years later, she realised that had been a fruitless exercise. He had been baffled, it felt almost weird. After all, he would never send anyone flowers. He'd rather put the money into a nice, new frying pan, which they needed.

For the first year, Billie showered Arun with love and affection, who, for the most part, enjoyed the attention. Billie knew she was putting more work into the relationship than Arun, but it felt right. Silly as it seemed, she believed in harmony and living happily ever after. She couldn't see how they would ever have the same problems that their friends experienced, and they didn't. But as the relationship lengthened, and Billie moved cities to be with Arun, she became frustrated that the love she gave didn't seem to be returned. Arun didn't think to stock the fridge with her favourite treats or consider where she wanted to go on holiday before he booked it. While Billie had fallen into the role of doing more of the household chores, she started to resent Arun's lack of participation. She was now a senior English teacher and work demanded more of her time. She began to feel unloved and unsupported. She had moved cities to be with him, damn it. She had moved Brandon away from his friends and his school. Arun continued to take many work trips and was oblivious to the hurt he was causing.

Bananas like Billie don't place demands on their partners but because they don't ask for what they want, they often don't get it. Every time Arun expressed his gratitude for something, Billie would say it was nothing and shrug it off, so he started to believe it was nothing.

Billie became more and more frustrated. Why didn't he notice she was upset? She thought her feelings should be obvious to Arun and her behaviour became passive aggressive. She clattered dinner plates on the table, slammed doors, and gave him the silent treatment. She said a sarcastic yes to everything and really meant no.

Unfortunately, Arun barely noticed. He was absorbed in his own life, having recently been promoted into a senior role. All that bottling up had to blow sometime, and when it did, Arun privately thought Billie was weak for not speaking up earlier and crying so much over their argument. (*Not a winner in the empathy stakes old mate, Arun).* Afterwards, he reflected that perhaps Billie had been a little off her game.

If Arun was more aware of Billie's nature and understood her fear of speaking up, he might have helped her broach the subject. If Billie knew Arun better, she would realise he likes direct, honest communication every time.

Billie had just heard that her best friend's elderly mother was gravely ill. She loved Mrs Jessop. She had been like a second mother and Billie had spent many childhood years at the Jessop house. Billie couldn't get Mrs Jessop out of her head. She imagined her in pain, she imagined her friend Trisha in her grief. And she talked about it. Arun, not so much. He didn't know Trisha's mother and didn't care, why waste his headspace? Billie's constant talking about this thing she saw as a problem was really getting on his nerves. She was even talking about flying halfway across the country for the funeral. Was she mad?

Billie applies the same empathic intensity to the domestic problems of her work friend Louise, and feels compelled to talk about it with Arun, who finds this more than irritating. He admits quietly to himself that he sometimes feels less respect for Billie for allowing other people's problems to become her issue.

As the years passed, Arun became more and more frustrated with Billie's lack of decision-making. In the early years, her inaction didn't bother him as much, but he needed some commitment from her. Billie loved being with Arun because he could make all the decisions for her. She made decisions all day at work and didn't need the pressure of making them at home as well. To Arun's ears, her replies of, 'Whatever you want,' or 'I don't mind,' made him want to scream.

Arun's parents were travelling from India to visit for the first time. He was keen to ensure they were comfortable, and, with their furniture in need of an upgrade, Arun found a new outdoor setting, lounge and sofa bed and consulted Billie, but she was stuck in indecision. At first Arun was exasperated, then he became angry. The more he ranted and raised his voice, the more Billie shut down. (*Pressure is not the winning strategy with a Banana.*) Finally, by explaining the impact her lack of decision-making was having on them, he was able to get through to Billie. He was also busy, and he was upset. Reassured of a return to harmony, Billie created time to choose the furniture.

The in-laws arrived and they loved Billie because she loved their son and they could see how happy he was. They were incredibly helpful when it came to improving Billie's life; while she was at work, they cleaned out the fridge and rearranged its contents; they repotted plants and moved them to a place where they'd thrive; and Arun's mother cooked not only the best butter chicken, but apparently, the best roast dinner, according to Arun. (*We can all see where this is heading, and it's not good.*)

It was their advice on the lack of discipline metered out to Brandon that finally tipped Billie over the edge. While his parents were out, she went for Arun over their comments, raising her voice to those levels of hysteria which meant he knew she was serious.

After four weeks with her in-laws, Billie's fuse had been on a long, slow burn. Now well and truly lit, the fire raged uncontrollably around their relationship. Oddly, Arun understands this type of behaviour. He shouts back. It gets ugly. And then the anger is gone; Billie is sorry, and Arun promises to keep Mother and Father out of her face.

One of Billie's biggest problems is supressing her anger. The anger begins slowly in her belly and every little incident adds to the gnarly lump of resentment which festers and grows until it explodes. Over time, she would learn to confront Arun more and more for a better, cleaner result. But this would be many years.

Arun struggled with Brandon from the very beginning. The kid was rude and disrespectful. He tried to teach Brandon about cars, about golf and sport, activities a boy should be interested in, but got nowhere. Why couldn't he just be sweet and adoring like his own nieces? He resented having to do the school pick up when Billie could not. He would ask Brandon how his day was and all he would get in response was, "good". The kid was a poor communicator. By the early teenage years, Arun often worked from home and he begrudged having to be there for Brandon when he arrived from school. And if Billie was out at one of her bloody charity things, he had to get Brandon dinner as well.

Arun put demands on Brandon and set him tasks he should have been able to achieve but rarely did. The kid had been babied, that was the problem, and Arun saw it as his job to correct it. Not only was Brandon Billie's son, he was her only child and the centre of her world. Brandon was not Arun's son, and he took time away he could be spending with his beloved Billie. He had never been good at sharing.

Arun's dilemma was compounded by his inability to have children. He refused to do IVF, considering this medical procedure demeaning and unnatural. Try as she might, Billie could not understand Arun's selfishness. Dismayed, she tried to counter every objection, but Arun would not budge. Her devastation turned to anger and, eventually, to a solution. Billie decided it would be great if they adopted a child from a developing country. Arun would rather poke hot needles in his eyes.

I'd like to tell you there was an easy answer to bringing a child into their family but the situation has too many variables. Perhaps surprisingly, Billie and Arun made it through. Brandon was influenced by Arun regardless, and at twenty-four has grown into a fine young man. It was often Arun who was there for him during the teenage years.

Now Head of the English Department, Billie's door was always open to staff members and their problems. She met with parents whenever they wanted to see her. She served on inter-school committees and attended every school football game and cooked sausages on the side. You see, everybody loved Billie and wanted a piece of her. Billie didn't look for reward. Her work was her reward and she found meaning through making others' lives better. She found it satisfying to be working with young people who were the future. Outside of work, she drove friends to the airport, fixed neighbours' gates, and helped friends' children with assignments.

She couldn't say no when someone asked for help and was the always the first to volunteer. She never deliberately drew attention to herself, but because of her public role at the school people noticed her good deeds. Still, friends and neighbours often took Billie's help for granted. She would come home late and just as she sat down for dinner the phone would ring. It would be someone with a problem. Forty minutes later when the call ended, the family had finished dinner and she would be left to eat alone. By the time the weekend came, she was exhausted and had no time left for her family. She was too busy going to all those sausage sizzles.

Billie had no time for herself. She didn't see this as selfless because she was powered by good intentions but her success and popularity in the community came at the expense of her family relationships.

Arun had long accepted he and Billie came from different planets. Caring about others was as natural as breathing for Billie and Arun simply struggled to understand this as a motivational form. What he did know was that he was obsessive in his love for her and oddly enough Brandon was sneaking into that category, and living her life this way gave her pleasure. He didn't like people taking advantage of Billie or how their own family time suffered. Billie's problem was, she just couldn't say no. Arun decided it was time to reassert control and insist on change. The truth was, Billie was exhausted and almost grateful for the intervention.

Together, they made a list of all Billie's extra activities and commitments and decided which were essential. Billie began working with a life coach to identify how she could be more efficient and still maintain her purpose. She realised her conversations were often too detailed and too lengthy, and learned how to save time on phone, email, and face-to-face meetings. Billie was able to find a compromise between what she gave others, to her family, and importantly, to herself.

Billie and Arun's relationship thrived over the years through acceptance and respect for each other's extreme differences. They have even taken on smidgens of each other's traits.

Billie has learned to speak up more at home, to assert herself, and make clear decisions. Arun has become a better listener, more sensitive to other's needs (*well, slightly more*), and more caring (*again, not going ahead in leaps and bounds here, but getting better*). Billie loves her strong, handsome Arun, the man she fell in love with who made her feel safe and secure. Arun knows he is deeply loved, and Billie is his own delicious Fruit he is careful not to bruise.

Banana and Apple

Despite their naturally opposing ways—intuition vs logic; empathy vs realism—the Banana's most common and successful pairing is with their diagonal opposite, the Apple. Bananas love that Apples seem to be everything they are not—driven, focused, and authoritarian, and able to do the strategic thinking for both. Apples love the perfect foil a Banana provides in support and helping them to relax.

Potential Problems

No partnership is perfect and the natural areas for this couple to clash centre on the Banana's idealism, their wish to be everyone's friend, their desire for an easy life, their perceived neediness and their propensity to run from confrontation. Bananas consider Apples' lack of compassion, absence of emotion, and aloofness to be problematic. Apples can be sceptical about romance and consider it something to be endured rather than enjoyed.

As Apples take control of everything, their Banana partners can often feel insignificant, and because they stay out of trouble and don't take risks, they don't seek the spotlight. They might not attract bad attention, but they may not get good attention either.

Billie and Mac: the Banana and the Mango

School teacher Billie had a run of bad boyfriends. They were too lazy, too needy, too controlling. She couldn't seem to get it right. Then she met Mac, who worked in the government, and there was an immediate attraction. He was handsome, strong, funny, and confident. Her social life increased one hundred-fold. Life was fun again. Billie has a seven-year-old son, Brandon. That was cool with Mac. He'd never been out with someone who had a child so it would be fun; a new challenge.

Billie gave out her love to Mac in bucket loads. It was the most natural thing in the world for her to hug regularly and say, 'I love you.' Occasions such as birthdays gave her the opportunity to spoil him with champagne and treats. To Mac, Billie seemed almost psychic, anticipating his needs before he realised them. He was in a constant state of bliss. A girl who adored him as much as he loved himself. Damn, life was good. He loved to create surprises for his wonderful Billie; dinner on a yacht, private picnics, concerts.

For the first few months, they were living in different cities and Billie did all she could to stay in touch. She called every day and sent flowers. Mac loved it. A girl who sent flowers; nice!

For the first year, Billie showered Mac with love and affection, and Mac spent money on wonderful experiences for Billie. She knew she was putting more emotional work into the relationship than Mac, but it felt right. Silly as it seemed, she believed in harmony and living happily ever after. She couldn't see how they would ever have the same problems that their friends experienced, and they didn't. But as the relationship lengthened, and Billie moved cities to be with Mac, she became frustrated that the love she gave just didn't seem to be returned in the same way. He seemed to love her by spending money.

Mac didn't think to stock the fridge with her favourite treats or consider where she wanted to go on holiday before he booked it. While Billie had fallen into the role of doing more of the household chores, she started to resent Mac's lack of participation. She was now a senior English teacher and work demanded more of her time.

Billie began to feel unloved and unsupported. She had moved cities to be with him, damn it. She had moved Brandon away from his friends and his school. Mac continued to take many work trips and was oblivious to the hurt he was causing.

Billie became more and more frustrated. Why didn't he notice she was upset? She thought her feelings should be obvious to Mac and her behaviour became passive aggressive. She clattered dinner plates on the table, slammed doors, and gave him the silent treatment. She said a sarcastic yes to everything but really meant no. Mac kind of noticed, but when he asked Billie what was wrong, she said nothing, and before long he had forgotten about it. He had recently been promoted into a senior role and was excited about the opportunities it opened up for him and for them as a couple. And every time Mac expressed his gratitude for something, Billie would say it was nothing and shrug it off, so he started to believe it was nothing.

All that bottling up had to blow. Poor Billie.

Bloody hell, thinks Mac, *I had no idea things had got so bad—why didn't she say anything? I can't believe she is so upset. Of course, I love her. What about the flowers and the presents?*

It seemed Billie wanted more time and more intimacy. Puzzled but keen to improve, he promised to change and was sincere in his promise. It would take a long time for Mac to improve, and he probably never reached the level Billie wanted. Billie needed to learn to speak up sooner, because Mac was willing to listen as long as she could keep his attention for long enough.

Billie had just heard that her best friend's elderly mother was gravely ill. She loved Mrs Jessop. She had been like a second mother and Billie had spent many childhood years at the Jessop house. Billie couldn't get Mrs Jessop out of her head. She imagined her in pain. She imagined her friend Trisha in her grief. And she talked about it. Mac was secretly bored with hearing about Mrs Jessup. He didn't know Trisha's mother and didn't care … why waste his headspace? So. Much. Talking. Still, he let Billie go on with it. He was skilled at turning off and letting his mind wander. If she needed to go to the funeral; go ahead, just don't make him go. Unless … Maybe they could tack on a trip to Margaret River? Now it's looking interesting …

Billie applies the same empathic intensity to the domestic problems of her work friend Louise. She loves to tell Mac all about her day, and although Mac tries to be interested, the constant chatter drives him barmy. (*Call your girlfriends, Billie, and save the big picture for Mac.*)

As the years passed, Mac becomes more and more frustrated with Billie's lack of decision-making. In the early years her inaction hadn't mattered as he made most of the decisions, from a new coffee table to a new cruise, Billie went along with whatever decision Mac made; she was so damned accommodating. He would love her to initiate ideas some of the time and push for what she wanted. In Billie's mind, she was initiating ideas. She managed the everyday detail; the grocery shopping, homework, activities and sport for Brandon, the household budget with its shared credit card. Early on, she had noticed that Mac didn't know what he spent, and she enjoyed helping him manage his money.

Billie loved being with Mac because he made all the other decisions for her. She made decisions all day at work and didn't need the pressure of making them at home as well. To Mac's ears, her replies of, 'Whatever you want,' or 'I don't mind,' made him want to scream. The thing was Billie really didn't mind.

Mac's parents were travelling from Scotland to visit for the first time. He wanted them to love his place and with a few things in need of an upgrade, Mac found a new outdoor setting, lounge, and sofa bed and consulted Billie, but she was stuck in indecision. Mac was exasperated because he likes to act, so he went ahead and bought everything. Billie was upset she hadn't had a say in the decision.

The in-laws arrived and they loved Billie because she loved their son and they could see how happy he was. They were incredibly helpful when it came to improving Billie's life; while she was at work, they cleaned out the fridge and rearranged its contents, they repotted plants and moved them to a place where they'd thrive, and Mac's mum cooked not only the best haggis but, apparently, the best roast dinner, according to Mac. (*We can all see where this is heading, and it's not good.*)

It was their advice on the lack of discipline metered out to Brandon that finally tipped Billie over the edge. While his parents were out, she went for Mac over their comments, raising her voice to a level of hysteria which meant he knew she was serious.

After four weeks with her in-laws, Billie's fuse had been on a long, slow burn. Well and truly lit, the fire raged uncontrollably around their relationship. Mac was stunned. After all, his parents were only trying to help. Was it possible Billie was being a bit dramatic? Her anger raged on until it burned out. Billie was sorry and Mac was sorry and he promised to keep Mum and Dad out of the way until the end of the trip.

One of Billie's biggest problems is supressing her anger. The anger starts slowly in her belly and every little incident adds to the gnarly lump of resentment which festers and grows until it explodes. Over time she would learn to confront Mac more directly for a more efficient result, and a lot less pain. But this would be many years later.

Mac loved Brandon. The kid was a bit introverted. He had obviously had a hard time because he could say things that weren't cool and started off clearly resenting Mac. But the kid had had to change schools and friends and was living in another house with another male, of course it was going to be a time of transition. It took a year or two, but after trying loads of different activities, Mac found a way to connect. Brandon loved fishing. So, after that it was fishing—from the beach, from kayaks, out with Mac's mate's offshore. The kid really opened up. When Billie had to work back late, he didn't mind picking up Brandon. Besides, it meant they could get pizza and watch shows on a streaming service that Billie didn't allow.

Mac couldn't wait to have his own family. If it was this good with someone else's son, imagine having your own! His balloon was cruelly burst when he discovered his low sperm count. Seriously? Him? Mr Attractive? IVF was the way to go then. There was always a solution. Many rounds later, Billie and Mac were blessed with twin baby girls.

What a perfect addition to their family. Mac felt useless when they were babies but once they started growing into little people, he was an active dad and excelled at playtime. For both, family relationships were precious. When the girls were small, Billie put every ounce of energy she had into loving and nurturing them, on top of the Banana love she heaped on Mac and Brandon. Mac was a good dad. He had a team of great staff now and things were running smoothly at work. In contrast, Billie's life was busier.

Now Head of the English Department, Billie's door was always open to staff members and their problems. She met with parents whenever they wanted to see her. She served on inter-school committees. She attended every school football game and cooked sausages on the side. Everybody loved Billie and wanted a piece of her. Billie didn't look for reward. Her work was her reward and she found meaning through making others' lives better. She found it satisfying to be working with young people who were the future. Outside of work, she drove friends to the airport, fixed neighbours' gates, and helped friends' children with assignments.

She couldn't say no when someone asked for help. She was the always the first to volunteer. She never deliberately drew attention to herself, but because of her public role at the school people noticed her good deeds. Still, friends and neighbours often took Billie's help for granted. She had come home late and just as she sat down for dinner the phone would ring. It would be someone with a problem. Forty minutes later when the call ended, the family had finished dinner and she would be left to eat alone. By the time the weekend came around, she was exhausted and had no time left for her family. She was too busy going to all those sausage sizzles.

Billie had no time for herself. She didn't see this as selfless, as she was powered by good intentions, but her success and popularity in the community came at the expense of her family relationships. For Billie, caring was as natural as breathing. Mac had long developed a technique for turning off when she talked about other people's problems. What he didn't like was when people took advantage of her and took too much time away from them. Billie's problem was, she just couldn't say no. His problem was their family was being neglected.

The family intervened to tell her how they felt. Not only did they feel a little unloved, but they were all worried about Billie's health. Billie was defensive. Her family were so privileged. They didn't need her like everybody else did! Mac had to draw on all his Mango charm. But it was the children who helped Billie over the line, to understand how her time away from them was affecting them as a family. They needed her. And that's something no Banana mother can ignore. Billie reluctantly put some parameters around times she took phone calls at night. And she recreated family night twice a week which they had always done when the girls were small. As a challenge to herself, Billie had to say no to at least one thing every week. Eventually Billie was able to find a compromise between what she gave others, what she gave her family, and what she gave to herself.

Billie and Mac lived happily ever after. (*You do know, that this phrase is a lie propagated in fairy tales, right?*) They have a deep love for each other and are strong relationship role models for their children. Mac the Mango insists on getting all the problems out on the table, and Billie the Banana has learnt it's not as scary to confront them as she once thought. Emotional maturity and acceptance of their differences has helped their relationship survive.

Banana and Mango

Bananas and Mangoes connect through their love of people. Both enjoy relationships and develop emotional ties easily. Both see the beauty in life. Bananas love the freedom and spontaneity a Mango partner can bring. Mangoes love the genuine warmth and love a Banana provides.

Potential Problems

Mango life is often considered too fast and too shallow for the Banana, who seeks a peaceful existence. Bananas would rather spend time relaxing with some binge TV and cups of tea, and the Mango needs to be more active every waking moment.

The differences in their pace of life creates additional issues for this pair. Mangoes always need to be engaged in an activity they consider interesting and can't understand the Banana's need to sit and do "nothing". Mangoes become frustrated, which impacts Bananas' self-esteem. While Mangoes appear confident, they hide a fragile ego and need recognition and reassurance for themselves before they can provide the emotional stability that a Banana needs.

Billie and Leo: the Banana and the Lime

School teacher Billie had a run of bad boyfriends. They were too lazy, too needy, too controlling. She couldn't seem to get it right. Then she met Leo, who worked in the government, and there was an immediate attraction. He was handsome, quiet, strong, and calm. Nothing was rushed. He decided what they would do and where they would go, and Billie didn't have to think it all.

Billie had a seven-year-old son, Brandon. Leo had always been nervous to get involved with someone else's child because he considered it fraught with danger. He had no parenting experience. He couldn't give someone else's child the love of a real parent. What if her child wasn't likeable? How would it all work? But his love for Billie overcame his anxiety. He had fallen for a goddess and would deal with the consequences later.

Billie gave out her love to Leo in bucket loads. It was the most natural thing in the world for her to hug regularly and say, 'I love you.' Occasions such as birthdays gave her the opportunity to spoil him with champagne and treats. To Leo, Billie seemed almost psychic, anticipating his needs before he realised them. She was some sort of angel. He loved looking after her too but could never match Billie's capacity to give in the relationship.

For the first few months, they were living in different cities and Billie did all she could to stay in touch. She sent Leo flowers. He wasn't quite sure how to take that. He was chuffed and a little embarrassed at the same time. After all, he didn't need everyone in the office to know his personal business. Billie showered Leo with love and affection, and Leo, a little shell-shocked, enjoyed the feeling of being so cherished.

Billie knew she was putting more work into the relationship than Leo, but it felt good. As silly as it seemed, she believed in harmony and happily ever after. She couldn't see how they would ever have the same problems that their friends experienced, and they didn't. But as the relationship lengthened, and Billie moved cities to be with Leo, she became frustrated that the love he gave didn't seem to be returned. Leo didn't think to stock the fridge with her favourite things treats or send her flowers. Okay, he did cook dinner, but it was always what he wanted to cook. While Billie had fallen into the role of doing more of the household chores, she started to resent Leo's lack of participation, especially now she was senior English teacher and work required more of her time.

Every time Leo expressed his gratitude for something, Billie would say it was nothing and shrug it off, so he started to believe it was nothing.

She began to feel unloved and unsupported. She had moved cities to be with him, damn it. She had moved Brandon away from his friends and his school. Leo was still having a great time, attending work events, and going away on trips.

Billie became more and more frustrated. Why didn't he notice she was upset? She thought her feelings were obvious to Leo and her behaviour became passive aggressive. She clattered dinner plates on the table, slammed doors, and gave him the silent treatment. She said a sarcastic yes to everything, but really meant no. Leo noticed Billie's behaviour but had no idea what to do. He thought he was giving back love in spades; more than he had ever done. He did all the household budgeting and did Billie's tax for her. That alone was worth a lot of loving. He kept the kitchen pantry organised, had spices and sauces in alphabetical order, and kept the plastics cupboard tidy because he noticed neatness wasn't her strong point. On her birthday, he sent her a list of links to different massage places for her to choose what she wanted. He didn't want to choose the wrong thing.

All that bottling up had to blow sometime, and when it did, Leo was astonished. Firstly, by her overly emotional exhibition and secondly that she felt unloved. How was that possible after all he does? There were tears from Billie, and indignation and bafflement from Leo. As soon as Billie got it off her chest, she realised she had allowed her emotions to build up and Leo really did love her—but could he please buy her flowers every now and again. (*Not from the supermarket, Leo, from a florist.*)

The misunderstanding was over, but Leo would not quickly forget. Could he have shown more love? Or was he completely in the right? Over the years, he spent a lot of time pondering how he could do things better.

Billie had just heard that her best friend's elderly mother was gravely ill. She loved Mrs Jessop. She had been like a second mother and Billie had spent many years at the Jessop house. Billie couldn't get Mrs Jessop out of her head. She imagined her in pain. She imagined her friend Trisha in her grief. And she talked about it. Being a sensitive soul himself, Leo knew Billie needed to get on a plane and visit Mrs Jessop. He did the sums and calculated they could use some of their rainy-day funds if she travelled at certain times, used the bus for airport transfers, and stayed with her friend. Billie applies the same empathic intensity to the domestic problems of her work friend Louise and can recall all the detail of every relationship she ever encountered. As a teacher this is a very handy quality.

The other drawback of all that empathy is for the Banana themselves. Billie takes on other peoples' problems to the point where she can lose sleep over them.

However, Leo enjoyed the stories she brought home from school and soon knew the cast of characters and their foibles as well as Billie. From an outburst from the principal to the sad story of a child who couldn't afford a school uniform, Leo was up for it. Dinner was always interesting listening to Billie rabbit on.

As the years went by, Leo became frustrated with Billie's easy-going nature. He had long ago assumed fiscal responsibility for the household, their holidays, their entire life really. He made careful, calculated decisions on everything from the purchase of a dining suite to choosing a financial advisor. If he couldn't make the right decision after much analysis, he would delay the decision. But Billie just didn't help.

Billie loved being with Leo because he made all the decisions. They were never made quickly, but they were made. Together they had been known to delay decisions for years. Back when he was single, Leo had visited Tahiti and brought back a perfect, single black pearl. When he met Billie, he wanted her to wear this beautiful pearl. He waited three or four years to make sure the relationship would work. Unfortunately, during that time, when he mentioned pearls to test the water, she unwittingly said she preferred the imperfect pearls.

The perfect black pearl stayed in the box for another few years. He had chosen this pearl so carefully and needed to make sure it would be appreciated. Finally, he showed it to her. To his relief, she loved it and couldn't wait to have it made into a ring. But Leo had planned for the pearl to be on a chain, to showcase the entire pearl. It seemed impossible they would ever reach a mutually acceptable decision. 20 years later, the perfect black pearl still sits alone in its box.

Leo's parents were travelling from South Australia to visit for the first time. It was critical they were comfortable and enjoyed his home, so to upgrade, Leo found a new outdoor setting, lounge, and sofa bed and consulted Billie, but she said she didn't mind what he chose. Leo found this incredibly frustrating. He had done the research, but he needed her to have an opinion. After all, she was part of this. From Billie's perspective, she thought he should sort it out as it was for his parents, and she was busy at school. Neither one of them liked conflict and the issues simmered for weeks as they sniped at each other, landing cheap shots.

Finally, Leo presented a prepared argument with a conciliatory tone. He explained the impact Billie's lack of decision-making was having on them; how he was busy too and this was upsetting him, which in turn affected the whole house. Reassured of a return to harmony, Billie created time to choose the furniture.

The in-laws, Ludwig and Anke, loved Billie because she loved their son and they could see how happy he was. They were incredibly helpful when it came to improving Billie's life. They pointed out how much water she wasted and collected bucket loads from the shower to water the plants. They explained how much electricity she wasted and turned appliances off at the power points. While she was at work, they cleaned out the fridge and rearranged its contents, with tips on how not to waste food. On top of all that, Leo's mother apparently cooked the best roast dinner, and her sponge cake had been voted by the Country Women's Association as the best at the show for several years running.

But it was their advice on the lack of discipline metered out to Brandon that finally tipped Billie over the edge. While his parents were out, she went for Leo over their comments, raising her voice to a level of hysteria which meant he knew she was serious. After four weeks with her in-laws, Billie's fuse had been on a long, slow burn. Well and truly lit, the fire raged uncontrollably around the relationship. Leo had not seen it coming. Well, he had, sort of. He knew what his parents were like but preferred to keep his head down, hoping it would all pass.

He rarely saw Billie like this and hated to see his lovely, calm Billie so upset. He was defensive, then sympathetic. Mum and Dad could be a bit much at times he told her, he would get them to back off. One of Billie's biggest problems is supressing her anger. The anger starts slowly in her belly and every little incident adds to the gnarly lump of resentment which festers and grows until it explodes.

Leo is better at raising issues, as long as he had time to prepare but before he reached that stage, he too had a gnarly lump of growing dissatisfaction. Over time, Billie learnt to approach Leo long before either of them reached boiling point.

When Brandon arrived in Leo's life, he represented massive change. In the six months before Billie moved in, Leo immersed himself in research on step parenting. He also worried himself sick about the house being kept tidy, privacy, schooling, Brandon's friends, and what seven-year-old boys eat.

As it turned out, co-parenting was not as frightening as he had thought. Although not painless, Billie was such a hands-on and caring mother, and so aware of Leo and his needs that she made all their lives so much easier. Leo could see bits of himself in Brandon if he was honest. He would ask how Brandon's day was and he'd reply, "good." That was Leo's response when he was a child and it brought back irritating memories of adults telling him he should learn to speak more.

The first time he had to prepare dinner for Brandon, Leo felt awkward, but over time they began to bond over meals when Billie worked late. He had more rules than Billie and insisted Brandon set and clear the table and clean up. Leo's rule was I cook, you clean. It worked for the two of them, but the dynamic changed when Billie was home, rushing to do everything for both. Leo quietly thought his way was better.

With Brandon in his life, Leo began to think about having a child of his own and was bitterly disappointed when he discovered he was infertile. While Billie was keen to try IVF or adopt, Leo spun deep into a well of angst and worry. He procrastinated around the cost, and had endless looping internal argument; *what if it doesn't work*? This went on for years and in the end, Billie bought two Labradoodles. Leo loved Gin and Tonic, focusing his efforts on them, and Brandon.

Now Head of the English Department, Billie's door was always open to staff members and their problems. She met with parents whenever they wanted to see her. She served on inter-school committees and attended every school football game and cooked sausages on the side. Everyone loved Billie and wanted a piece of her. Billie didn't look for reward. Her work was her reward and she found meaning through making others' lives better. She found it satisfying to be working with young people who were the future. Outside of work, she drove friends to the airport, fixed neighbours' gates, and helped friends' children with assignments.

She couldn't say no when someone asked for help and was always the first to volunteer. She never deliberately drew attention to herself, but because of her public role at the school people noticed her good deeds. Still, friends and neighbours often took Billie's help for granted. She would come home late and just as she sat down for dinner, the phone would ring. It would be a friend or someone with a problem. Forty minutes later when the call ended, the family had finished dinner and she would be left to eat alone. By the time the weekend came around, she was exhausted and had no time left for her family. She was too busy going to all those sausage sizzles.

Billie had no time for herself. She didn't see this as selfless as she was powered by good intentions but her success and popularity in the community came at the expense of her family relationships.

Leo tolerated this for a long time. After all, this was Billie. She was a giver. But as Brandon grew up and had his own life, Leo became increasingly lonely. He tried to raise his loneliness with Billie, but Billie waved it off. Eventually it was an old friend of Billie's who gave her a loving but direct Mango hit between the eyes. If she didn't stop being Saint Billie to the world, she would lose her beloved Leo.

Billie was exhausted from all that giving. She wasn't as young and energetic as she used to be and taking on everyone else's emotional problems was incredibly draining. At first, she couldn't see how she could eliminate any of her responsibilities. She felt she simply didn't have enough time in the day, but her Mango mate was happy to tell her she talked too much, in too much detail, and for too long. She could save many hours a week right there. And she needed to learn to say no. Being unable to say no was at the heart of Billie's poor time management and it wasn't only a desire to help others; sometimes she said yes when she really wanted to say no.

The transition was difficult for Billie because she had to learn to say no. She started with the least scary people and worked her way up to the principal. She was able to find a compromise between what she gave others, what she gave her family, and what she gave to herself. Billie and Leo lived a long and happy life together.

Billie loves Leo like only a Banana can with every fibre of her being. He is her rock, her steady, constant supporter quietly cheering from the sidelines, providing stability and harmony in their home. Leo still thinks of Billie as his beautiful goddess and feels blessed she chose him. She brings sunshine and peace into his world.

Banana and Lime

Bananas and Limes are a comfortable mix. They are kind and patient and keep a good home together. They cultivate a genuine and regular circle of friends. The Banana is happy to have the Lime organise the house and together they seek stability, security, and peace. Limes feel secure about Bananas' moral values and sensitivity. They never feel threatened and are always supported.

Potential Problems

Bananas need romance and the pragmatic Limes can lose patience with more impractical notions. The sensitive Lime is not without romance but their logical, pragmatic side often wins out, making it appear that they're not connecting. This can leave the Banana feeling unloved and unappreciated.

Limes can become frustrated with Bananas' casual attitude to life. Bananas don't exactly break the rules, but they often don't bother with them. The car doesn't always need to be washed on Saturdays and being late every now and again is okay.

Billie and Brad: the Double Banana

School teacher Billie had a run of bad boyfriends. They were too lazy, too needy, too controlling. She couldn't seem to get it right. Then she met Brad, who worked in the government, and there was an immediate attraction. He was handsome, strong, and so damned nice. It was a relief to be with someone who was so easygoing.

Billie had a seven-year-old son. She was always a bit worried telling men about Brandon because they often walked away. By the age of seven, children have passed the cute stage, but she needn't have worried. Brad was neither thrilled nor repelled. He was happy with whatever Billie wanted to sling his way.

Billie gave out her love to Brad in bucket loads. It was the most natural thing in the world for her to hug regularly and say, 'I love you.' Occasions such as birthdays gave her the opportunity to spoil him with champagne and treats. To Brad, Billie seemed almost psychic, anticipating his needs before he realised them. He couldn't believe how lucky he was.

For the first few months, they were living in different cities. This was unbearable for both and they were in touch several times a day. They sent gifts. Surprises. Turned up unexpectedly. It was a whirlwind and a relief to finally move in together. This was the first time Billie had felt her partner was putting an equal amount of work into the relationship. They were showering each other with love and affection. (*Stop puking, Apples. Oh, right, you won't be reading this bit because it's not about you!*)

It seemed both Billie and Brad believed in harmony and happily ever after. Billie couldn't see how they would ever have the same problems that their friends experienced, and they certainly didn't. These two Bananas had their own unique problem with all the giving. Both felt guilty being on the receiving end of so much giving and neither felt deserving of all the love. So, they tried to outdo one another to ease their own guilt. (*We can all see how ridiculous this is going to get*). Billie kept Brad's favourite foods in the house. Brad cooked Billie's favourite meals. Billie knew Brad liked a certain brand of deodorant and made sure he never ran out. Brad put posies of flowers next to Billie's bed. Billie booked a night at Brad's favourite restaurant; Brad booked a cruise to their favourite island. It became so routine that even though one of them might be exhausted, they felt it was their turn, and climbed the giving hill one more time.

Their competitiveness began to devalue the love they had for each other. Even they could see the craziness and they realised it didn't make them love each other more. They agreed to pull back, and more importantly, to try and accept the giving with grace, without needing to give in return.

Neither one of them stressed too much about the house. If they didn't clean up much after dinner it was no big deal.

Admittedly, the laundry tended to pile up on the floor and it took days to put away their clothes. The dog roamed freely, leaving dog hair all over the furniture, but friends were always assured of a genuine welcome if they popped in unexpectedly.

Billie and Brad's laid-back approach extended to household administration. They managed to get the bills paid on time but neither were too fussed on keeping receipts or warranty cards. It wasn't until they were robbed, they discovered that they had never organised contents insurance. Still, they had each other and their health, so what did it matter they lost a couple of laptops and a few pieces of jewellery? Both were casual about money as well. They both made a reasonable wage and didn't live extravagant lives. Both had superannuation so didn't worry about their retirement. They didn't invest in property or shares; they were simply happy to have enough to live on each day.

Billie and Brad were both sought after friends as they are always willing to listen to someone else's problems. No wonder their friends pop in as often as they do.

Volunteer work was a focus in their lives. They had their own separate charities but also entered fun runs and other events in support of a good cause, and were the first to donate when a work colleague was fund raising for charity. Once a month, they worked in a soup kitchen together.

Billie had just heard that her best friend's elderly mother was gravely ill. She loved Mrs Jessop. She had been like a second mother to her and she'd spent many years at the Jessop house. Into adulthood, that had not changed. Mrs Jessop had become Marg, and now Marg was dying. Billie couldn't get it out of her head. She imagined her in pain. She imagined her friend Trisha in her grief. She imagined the wrench of losing her own mother. And she talked about it. She needed to get on a plane and go see her friend. For Brad it was a no brainer. Just go! He couldn't bear the pain himself.

Brad's parents were travelling from Melbourne to visit for the first time. To make sure they were comfortable and so he wouldn't hear complaints, Brad wanted to buy a new outdoor setting, lounge, and sofa bed. They both knew they needed new furniture, but they seemed like big decisions and neither one of them had the head space. Life got in the way and they found themselves still without the furniture the weekend before Brad's parents' visit. Galvanised into action, they went to the furniture store. They found an outdoor setting, no problem. The lounge and sofa bed proved a little trickier so they ended up buying whatever could be delivered on time. The lounge arrived the day before. They had done it. Except neither had taken accurate measurements and the lounge didn't fit the space. They had to turn it on it an angle. It blocked the kitchen door a bit but that would be okay.

The in-laws arrived and they loved Billie because she loved their son and they could see how happy he was. And she was such a sweet thing. But. Billie's mother-in-law thought, *Oh my lord! What a place they lived in! This is all Billie's doing really because Bradley knows better. Sleeping on a sofa bed! What was she thinking? They hadn't done that, since, well, never. And the lounge! It was too big for the room. It didn't fit.*

Sloppy housekeeping really. It certainly didn't reflect Bradley's upbringing. Brad's mother felt the need to vacuum and clean immediately on her arrival. *And the poor girl couldn't really cook, could she?* Brad's mother expertly whipped up all his favourite meals and put them in the freezer for when she wasn't there.

Even Billie, with the patience and empathy of a saint, was being pushed to her limit. She loved her home and didn't like the suggestion it wasn't up to scratch. She didn't want to upset Brad on his parents' visit so she packed away her feelings so no-one would see she was upset. That was until Brad's mother decided to pass on some expert advice on parenting that Billie was apparently unaware of. Billie blew. While his parents were out, she went for Brad over their comments, raising her voice to a level of hysteria he had never heard before.

Brad's parents had stayed with them for four weeks and Billie's fuse had been on a long, slow burn. Well and truly lit, the fire raged uncontrollably around the relationship. Brad was shocked but not surprised. His own empathy gene had kicked in early and he had constantly asked Billie if she was okay. Why then did she reply yes? Rivers of tears later, Billie was spent, and Brad knew he had to confront his mother. It took a day or two, because confrontation was not his strength. But he did it. The next day his father had an emergency back in Melbourne, and home they went.

One of Banana Billie's biggest problems is supressing her anger. The anger starts slowly in her belly and every little incident adds to the gnarly lump of resentment which festers and grows until it explodes. Brad had the same challenge but hadn't quite realised it until he witnessed Billie's explosion. They hadn't experienced it between them because their world was so calm and steady. They simply didn't have arguments. If they disagreed, one was always quick to accommodate the other and move on. But they agreed they could both learn to manage this better in their own workplaces. They needed to speak up more before it got to blow out stage.

As people lovers, Billie and Brad's social lives centred around a wide group of friends and children and their own volunteer work. But during the week, their conversation often went something like this:

Brad: What would you like to do tonight?

Billie: I don't mind. What would you like to do?

Brad: I don't mind. Dinner out?

Billie: I don't mind. Maybe Thai?

Brad: I don't mind. Whatever you want.

Because they didn't mind so much, they often stayed in. It was a happy life.

Brad was cool with having Brandon in his life. He wasn't a bad kid. It was nice to have him around, to kick a footy with or hang out together. And as Billie's work became more demanding it really was no problem to pick him up from school or help with homework. Not that he really did much of that. Billie was one of the current breed of teachers who believed that kids worked hard enough during the day, why pressure him too much at home?

He couldn't wait to have a family of his own so with the news he couldn't naturally have children, Brad was hit hard. He and Billie spent many tearful hours talking through their options. In the end it seemed the only logical solution was to adopt. After all, so many babies came into the world who couldn't be cared for by their own parents. The process was not short but was somewhat simpler to help children from developing countries. A few years later, they had a beautiful baby girl from South Korea and a little boy from Colombia, both wrapped up in a huge bunch of Banana love.

While they were waiting for their adopted children, Billie and Brad joined a foster parent program and fostered many children over the years, often having up to eight children in their home at a time. Some stayed for just a few nights, needing immediate safety and care, others were with them for a month. Two of them arrived as teenagers and stayed to become part of the family.

Together Billie and Brad had boundless empathy, love, and care to give. They willingly shared what they had and ensured all their children, whether Billie's son Brandon, their adopted children, or their foster children, were treated fairly and equally. Their children may not have learned systems and general tidiness, but they learned to care, to share, and to give.

As time went on, Brad's loyal and dedicated team meant he had the flexibility to work more at home, just as Billie's career began more demanding. Now Head of the English Department, her door was always open to staff members and their problems. She met with parents whenever they wanted to see her. She served on inter-school committees. She attended every school football game and cooked sausages on the side. Everybody loved Billie and wanted a piece of her. Billie didn't look for reward. Her work was her reward and she found meaning through making others' lives better. She found it satisfying to be working with the young people who were the future. Outside of work, she drove friends to the airport, fixed neighbours' gates, and helped friend's children with assignments.

She couldn't say no when someone asked for help and was always the first to volunteer. She never deliberately drew attention to herself, but because of her public role at the school, people noticed her good deeds. Still, friends and neighbours often took Billie's help for granted. As their children were older now, Billie knew Brad was there for them so she had unwittingly created more time for other people than she had for her own family.

She would come home late, and just as she sat down for dinner, the phone would ring. It would be a friend, or someone with a problem. Forty minutes later when the call ended, the family had finished dinner and she would be left to eat alone. By the time the weekend came, she was exhausted and had no time left for her family. She was too busy going to all those sausage sizzles. In her earnest drive to help others, Billie was happy not to think of herself which in turn included her family. She would fall into bed each night content in the knowledge that she was living a life of service.

Billie had no time for herself. She didn't see this as selfless, as she was powered by good intentions, but her success and popularity in the community came at the expense of her family relationships. One night, she finished a long phone call helping solve someone else's problem and went straight to bed without dinner. She told Brad she just couldn't do it anymore and ended up spending several days in bed. Suffering from exhaustion and the common Banana affliction of never saying no and giving too much, she had burned herself out. So many children, a demanding career, and a whole bunch of people who sucked the energy out of her had proved too much.

As Billie's health improved, she and Brad hatched a plan. There was no doubt their children came first. She needed to work but she could cut down on the volunteering and she could start saying no. Simply, no. A younger Billie would it have found this thought unfathomable but now it seemed right. In fact, saying no was so empowering, she wished she'd started saying it sooner. Billie was able to find a compromise between what she gave others, what she gave her family, and what she gave to herself. Only a Banana would have this problem.

Billie and Brad have an unbreakable bond. Over the years they have always worked towards the same goals, driven by values and not by money. Their lives were never grandiose and in retirement, they made do with what they had. Billie loves her strong, handsome Brad, the man who loved her back in the way she wanted to be loved. They've supported each other, weathered storms, and argued little. Life together is stable and content.

Two Bananas together

Two Bananas in a relationship have a peaceful, harmonious existence. They won't argue over which TV program to watch or which social invites to accept. It's deeply satisfying for them to share the same world and enjoy each other's steadiness and low stress lifestyle.

Potential Problems

The potential trouble is that they may each tire of the narrow focus they have created as their world. Without the right outside stimulation, Bananas can become bored with each other. One will seem to be more clingy or needy than the other and the other's second dominant preference emerges and becomes irritated at what they perceive as weakness.

Bananas can also get quite uncomfortable with other's giving. They can feel guilty, as if they don't deserve so much kindness, and feel they must give back which devalues what the other partner is trying to give. The challenge is for each to learn to graciously accept when the other is giving.

Bananas' stress-free nature can backfire when it comes to household administration. They can't be bothered with receipts and warranty cards and nobody can find the insurance policy or even remember if it's been paid. Someone needs to be in control.

How to Handle the Banana in your life

One of Bananas' biggest complaints is that people don't listen to them. They often feel ignored or talked over because they refuse to dominate a conversation. Avoid getting to this point and become more aware of their personal needs and always make time to listen.

They get enjoyment from pleasing, so accept it and try not to reject it. Try also to find a balance with all that taking. Perhaps you can give back more, though with a Banana, you will need to insist. Don't take all their attention for granted and assume they have no needs of their own. Though they give without keeping score, it's only natural they'll want some love in return. Tap into what's important to them. They may be hesitant to ask you for favours or help. By increasing your awareness of their needs, you can try to anticipate them, and encourage your Banana to speak freely.

The more extreme the Banana, the more they will tell you what you want to hear, so make sure you find out what their real opinions are. When you say, 'Let's go white-water rafting on the Zambezi!' you may hear 'Sure!' If you could get inside their head you'd hear, *Awesome. Something I never wanted to do. Ever.*

When your Banana says they don't want to go to the movies, it may mean, 'I don't want to go to the movies if it takes you away from tennis with your friends, but I'd really like to go to the movies.' Learn to listen for more than what's said and encourage them to speak directly. Watch for your Banana's limitations. Their trouble spots include having their feelings easily hurt, taking on too much, being easily discouraged, and their fear of speaking up assertively. Help with this, but don't condemn them for it.

When you do clash, ask yourself if they are causing the issue or if it's a clash of values. You may believe in living every minute in what you see as a productive way, while they may consider bingeing on a new drama series is productive because it helps them to relax.

When you criticise a Banana without care, it leads to self-doubt and blame on their part. It's an automatic reaction for them to take the blame. Stop it right now. It's unhealthy behaviour for both of you. Think carefully before you speak and make sure that if you give kind, constructive criticism, you balance it out with plenty of praise. Watch for nonverbal signs that your Banana is upset. Choose your words, your tone, and your own body language thoughtfully for the most effective communication when your Banana is feeling tense. Don't try to fix how they're feeling. Don't be domineering, demanding, or controlling. Don't put them in overly confrontational situations. And don't forget to say thank you.

Tips for Bananas

Every time you are about to offer help that will put you out, stop and consider what's in it for you. Ask yourself if the help is wanted or needed. There's no point in turning up with a rich beef casserole for a friend who's just had a baby if she's vegetarian. If someone says thank you, don't shrug it off as if it's not important. If you do this, others will find themselves agreeing your good deed is not such a big deal. They won't value your gesture and you will think you're not appreciated. Not a win for you. Learn to ask for help and learn to accept it. Instead of feeling guilty when something nice happens to you, practice saying, 'I deserve this.'

When someone asks for your opinion, think about the topic and have an answer. Don't be fearful about whether that opinion is right or wrong: it is simply your opinion. Be confident with it. Develop your own activities so you don't depend solely on your partner to provide your social life. If you're known to procrastinate, try getting started on the task. It can be easier than facing a daunting or disagreeable task all at once. And remember decision-making is one of life's essential survival skills. Practice it.

Be aware that you avoid confrontation and practice stepping up to it. Speak up, even if it feels difficult, and express your anger or frustration directly. It's fine to say something negative about a situation without feeling guilty or bad for the other person. Likewise, not all criticism is directed at you. Learn not to take everything personally. Your idea of harmony might be different to others. But your fear of confrontation is the very thing that causes disharmony with some people, mainly Apples and Mangoes, who see it as a weakness.

Don't apologise just to keep the peace, and listen for the amount of times you say 'I'm sorry' in one day. Banish the minor issues and focus on apologies for the big mistakes.

When one relationship ends, hold back from rushing headlong into the next. It's healthy to experience life as your own person, on your own, doing your own thing, and just looking after you.

Short and Sweet

Bananas in a relationship

- have an idealistic and romantic view of love
- need reassurance and for love to be expressed
- create a warm home
- anticipate your needs and gain satisfaction from pleasing you
- sensitive to your moods
- suffer guilt easily
- don't place many demands
- can't say no
- fear conflict and speaking their mind
- dependable and stable.

Banana sticking points

- moody
- unforgiving when betrayed
- offer to help everyone and become overloaded at their own and their family's expense
- need to be loved in return
- easily hurt
- take things personally
- lack decision-making skills
- overly controlling partners spell disaster.

Mixed Fruit

Banana-Apple: Bananas love Apples' drive, focus, and authority; Apples love Bananas' support and the help to relax. Bananas are frustrated by Apples' control and lack of emotion. Apples are frustrated by Bananas' idealism and neediness.

Banana-Mango: Both love people. Bananas love Mangoes' freedom and spontaneity; Mangoes love Bananas' genuine warmth. Bananas are frustrated by the pace and lack of depth in Mango life, while Mangoes have no time for the emotional support a Banana needs.

Banana-Lime: Both share a common pace. Bananas love Limes' organisation, security, and peace; Limes love Bananas' sensitivity, moral values, and peace. Bananas get frustrated by Limes' rules and pragmatism. Limes get frustrated by Bananas' casual attitude.

Two Bananas: Both share a peaceful existence. Both can become bored with each other and frustrated with trying to give, and no-one does the administration chores.

Handling a Banana

- increase your awareness of your Banana's needs
- listen to them
- pull back on controlling them
- don't reject the things they do for you
- don't take their attention for granted
- lose nasty criticism and replace it with loving feedback
- listen hard for their real opinions
- They may often tell you what they think you want to hear.

Tips for Bananas

- reduce the number of times you say, 'I don't care what we do' or, 'I don't mind'
- develop your own interests
- don't dismiss it when someone says thank you
- learn to accept compliments
- try partial tasking if you're prone to procrastination
- take baby steps for bigger jobs
- check yourself every time you offer to help others
- don't fear confrontation—speak up, it can be useful
- don't take everything personally
- stop the guilt on everything
- ask for help
- accept help
- only apologise for important things you really are sorry for
- try being on your own for a while if a relationship breaks up.

PART THREE

FRUIT SALAD

Chapter 11

A Fruity Family Christmas

It's a time of year many of us dread because we're often thrown together with people we know through blood or marriage, but not always through choice. And so, it was the diverse Berry family came together to celebrate Christmas.

With a string of Christmases past lurching from mediocre to, frankly, disastrous, Annette and Archie decided to take control. This year they would be in neutral territory; they'd rented a bright, spacious, and very expensive beach house.

This Christmas, all the grandchildren were overseas so it would be an all-adult gathering. Annette's brother Liam and sister Billie were bringing their partners, respectively, Lana and Leo. Only brother Mitch was missing. He and his space cadet wife Mel were now living in Nicaragua. *Clever move,* Annette thinks, *far away from all this.*

Mum, Betty, and Dad, Alan, are coming of course. They never miss a chance to see the family they've created. *Always lovely to see Mum—just wish she'd stand up more to Dad.*

As an added bonus, they had Annette's ex Marty; because after all, he is the father of her children, and fairly likeable. The wild card was Leo's parents, who Annette had not met, visiting from the country. Then there was Annette and Archie. Eleven of them. What could possibly go wrong?

Annette was excited about Christmas, and let's face it, she and Archie put on the best get-togethers. As Apples, they have the control they enjoy, along with Annette's inner Mango planning the party at big picture level and Archie's inner Lime there to manage the detail. Although, with her darling brother Liam on hand, whose expertise in detail extends to vacuuming his balcony and keeping a spreadsheet for his wardrobe, there is little left to do, so Archie's Lime is barely needed.

Archie agreed to the family get together on the condition it was not in his home. He doesn't like anyone staying at their home, least of all Annette's family. His visitor policy is one night only. Liam was the official Catering Captain and had organised contributions from everyone. Under Annette's approval, of course.

Annette had pre-ordered the Christmas tree because of course you must have a living tree. Not keen to drive almost an hour to collect the tree, she used her Apple coercion and Mango charm to persuade the Pickup Only guys to deliver for a price. Everybody has a price.

The tree looked magnificent because Annette had been able to decorate it herself without the addition of the extended family's sentimental childhood decorations that did nothing for the coastal chic Hamptons look she was going for. She was also pleased that, at Betty's insistence, they'd all agreed to give money to the local children's charity rather than spend it on gifts because really, no-one would have managed to colour code their gift wrapping and it all ends up quite messy and out of control.

Having settled in the suite with the ocean view, Annette and Archie waited for the family to arrive.

Christmas Eve

The consistently punctual Liam and Lana were the first. They'd rather give up a week's wages than be late, Annette thought. Always pleased to see her baby brother, Annette rushes in with a hug. Then she turned, armed with a bright smile, and planted an obligatory kiss on her sister-in law's cheek. *God she was cold, this one*, thought Annette.

The truth was, Annette found Lana a sap. She suffered from resting miserable face and was quick to criticise but never stepped up for a good argument. And she was a bloody vegan for God's sake and lactose intolerant. Still, *no French cheese for you*, Annette thought gleefully. She instructs Archie to show them to their room.

Liam immediately felt his sister's lack of warmth. He was so worried about Annette picking on Lana, she always did and Lana never stood up for herself. She would just go quiet and impossible. He was stressed already! *No, no, relax, everything is going to be fine*. He would manage Lana. And Annette.

The parents arrived next in the latest model luxury car. Alan and Betty had worked hard to give their children private educations and raise them well. They were proud of all of them. Annette with her own law firm, Liam with his interior design business, Wilhelmina was now head of English and Drama at an exclusive school. Mitchell, well, he was their free spirit.

They played their roles well. Alan, the smooth and charming patriarch, believed he ruled the family with a firm and fair hand, but in truth, he used *Game of Thrones* as his playbook. Betty, a lovely woman who kept a good home, had been chosen as his glamourous wife all those years ago when he was building up the firm. *She married well,* he thought.

Betty privately noted that Annette and Archie had, in their usual form, taken the best room for themselves. She smiled as she handed Archie their luggage to take to their room.

Their youngest daughter, who insisted on being called Billie, flew in the door, arms laden with gifts, her sweet husband Leo lugging the bags. They had brought that damned dog with them too. He had a lovely nature, but he was not well behaved. And here were Leo's parents. *Good Lord. Country people. What is she wearing? And what is with all the eskies?* thought Betty.

Leo's parents had come armed with produce from their farm they had carefully packed and carried all the way from South Australia. Eskies full of potatoes, pumpkins, endless bags of kale, cherries. Ludwig unpacked his very own market stall as he explained the origins of each fruit and vegetable and detailed how his seed program enabled him to provide potatoes in December.

Annette's bright smile, which is known as her Christmas smile, was a little tight as, at Anke's insistence, she manoeuvred the world's largest cauliflower into her overstuffed fridge. Leo observed, as he always did. He did not want Billie's uppity family looking down their noses at his genuine, hardworking parents.

As the heat of the day dropped, the family settled in for afternoon drinks and nibbles. Although she was an excellent cook, Billie had been delegated to chips and dips, heaven forbid the youngest sibling might be capable of anything trickier. Leo had told her to protest but she didn't like to upset the Annette and Liam applecart. As they were taking their first sips and engaging in the polite, hesitant conversation you make when some in the group are not well known, they hear noise in the hallway. Marty has arrived. Late. What a surprise.

'Hey, everybody—I'm here!' Launching into the group larger than life, Marty hugs everyone, including Anke, much to her consternation, and pulls out several bottles of French champagne. *I told you we should have bought French*, Lana hisses at Liam. In the hallway, he presents Annette with a giant wreath made of green and red balloons.

Oh dear, Annette sighs, *where to put this? My colour scheme is Byron Bay rattan with gold and white trim.* Christmas smile.

When everyone had settled around the huge living area, Anke presented her contribution to the gathering. Although she and Ludwig were second generation Australians, they still enjoyed their German heritage and had bought a Christmas Stollen and Lebkuchenherzen. *Brilliant*, thinks Annette, *those horrible gingerbread hearts with hard icing that no-one likes. What the hell will I do with those?* But wait. Anke's pièce de résistance is a traditional English Christmas pudding she made. Ta da!

Everyone holds their breath. Liam *always* made the pudding—every year—it was his thing. Each October he agonised, unsure it would work out, and every year it was a triumph. Annette made dessert which is a stunning mango and macadamia nut trifle and now, here was an uninvited pudding, sitting alone on the pouffe.

The pause in conversation stretched awkwardly. Annette offered a polite thank you. Liam said nothing. Archie and Alan enjoyed the discomfort. Lana thought, *fantastic, yet another thing for Liam to stress about.* Leo felt sick for his mother and felt the beginnings of a lump of distaste for the whole Berry family—except for his beloved Billie—start to fester.

Billie rushes in, unable to bear the tension. 'Anke wins awards for her cooking you know. For years, her date scones have won at the show in Mt Barker. She is a celebrated baker! What a treat this will be! You'll love it.'

But it was too late. Anke's eyes had narrowed. 'I can give it to someone else who'll appreciate it.'

In the end it was Marty the Mango who came to the rescue. 'Let's go to the pub!'

'Brilliant idea,' they all agreed.

Relieved that the tension had eased, Annette is reminded why she once loved Marty.

Damn it, Archie thinks, *I wanted to see more of a showdown. Maybe tomorrow.*

As they all packed up, Billie noticed Ludwig and Anke sitting on the couch. 'We'd prefer to watch the Christmas Carols on TV, thank you very much.' Billie's heart sank. She knew Leo was looking forward to the pub. She smiled at him then sighed and sat down with the in-laws, who thought she wasn't quite good enough for their son, and watched the carols.

I'm so lucky to have her, Leo thought, *I really must get that black pearl made into a ring.*

No-one noticed the dog munching on the Stollen.

Christmas Lunch

Anke had never quite accepted Billie. Her housekeeping was negligent. She had failed to give their son Leo his own child.

She was useless at disciplining her own son let alone the dog. The dog should be put down, or at least sent to the pound. She was secretly glad he was sick from all that fruit.

Under Liam's watchful eye, Lana had been tasked with peeling the vegetables. Billie and Leo were keen to help but neither was allowed, having been identified as inferior at the task, despite having, professionally, a combined number of 120 staff reporting to them.

Annette was swanning around showing off her chilled cucumber and prawn soup with crispy prawn heads while Betty oohed and aahed. Billie earned a sympathetic smile for her tasty dip and selection of chips. Suspicious of the fancy food, Ludwig and Anke ate only the cherries they brought with them.

The carving of the Ham was always going to be cause for concern. Annette believed, as the host of the event, it was Archie's job. Alan, as patriarch of the family naturally believed the task would fall to him. While the debate continued, Marty, fuelled by a couple of solid early morning Bloody Marys, picked up a knife to just get the damn thing started.

His enthusiastic hacks were met with horror and Betty, surprisingly, took Ludwig aside and asked him to take over. He beamed at her. Alan's usual overly confident presence became a little more aggressive.

Unfortunately, Ludwig's careful and methodical ham carving took so long that Lana's champagne consumption, coupled with her propensity for hypoglycaemia, sparked targeted sniping at Liam—the perfect son. No-one sees the stress he brings. No-one sees how boring he is.

Alan can't stand the sluggish carving of the ham pace and pushes Ludwig aside. Mortified, Betty tries to stand up for Ludwig. Alan delivers a chilling reminder that Betty has no place being involved. Ludwig is relieved Anke is in the shower.

As they were preparing to plate up, there was a sharp knock on the door. Billie jumped up and opened it with a shriek of delight. Into the room comes the missing link, Mitch and his wife Mel, home from Nicaragua. 'We couldn't let you lot have Christmas without us!'

Filling the room with their energy and excitement there was a flurry of activity to find space at the table. 'We can only stay one night so let's enjoy!'

Liam felt his cortisol levels rising. Mitch the show off. Mitch the favourite who does nothing for Mum and Dad all year, turns up out of the blue and gets all the attention. He and his stupid wife swan in for a night, be the life of the party, and leave. The Christmas food, timed to the minute for perfectly roasted meats, simmering gravy and hot vegetables, was now growing cold on their plates. He could feel his heart rate elevating, palms sweating, and mouth going dry; just like the meat.

He shares his fears with Lana who scoffs at him. As a vegan she has only eaten the dip and even that was average. She does, however, have a pleasant glow from Marty's champagne, not Liam's Aussie sparkling. He notices she is laughing a bit too enthusiastically with Alan. *Hang on, is she flirting? With Dad??* Christmas is turning into a disaster!

The meal is delayed 40 minutes as the newcomers settle in and regale the family with their travel tales. Leo helps Annette and Liam, who covers the steaming food trays and feelings with foil.

Throughout the meal, Ludwig mutters to himself as he pushes food around his plate. He is a simple man with simple needs—*why aren't the vegetables cooked properly?* The gravy isn't how Anke makes it and the meat isn't cooked through—it's raw! Who serves salads alongside a roast dinner and what is that rabbit food anyway? Worst of all, the food is not hot. Anke makes soothing noises and agrees. This is not the way to serve a Christmas meal.

Leo is stressed. His parents are clearly not fitting in and he is frustrated at not having an assigned job, so he's taken it upon himself to keep the table clean and tidy. An enthusiastic organiser, he removes plates while others are still eating, more than once. He refills water glasses, replaces serviettes, and wonders—not for the first time—how an accomplished man holding down a senior role for the nation's corporate watchdog ended up as the water glass guy at Christmas. This family has never taken him seriously.

Conversation has moved to the forthcoming election and opinions fly across the table. There are the climate change activists and the coal mining supporters, those who believe in letting everyone into the country, and those who, vehemently, don't. But mainly it is Alan, Archie, and Annette airing their views and enjoying the opportunity to spar. Marty is interested for a moment, but is soon distracted by the fun exploits of Mitch and Mel. Ludwig and Anke, after venturing their thoughts, realise they are in the minority and politely say nothing more. Lana is more interested in her glass, and Billie, Betty, Leo, and Liam try to steer the conversation towards safer terrain.

After lunch, Mitch sets up a board game to pass the afternoon, and Annette suggests teaming up in pairs because she knows she and Archie will win. Alan retreats to his room, ostensibly to have a nap but truthfully to be away from the dour Anke and her milksop husband. Betty happily agrees to be Marty's partner. She has always liked Marty.

The game starts with fresh zeal as Mitch and Marty organise a round of shots. Leo, who by this time has had his mother insulted, her Stollen destroyed, eaten lukewarm food, and endured superficial conversation thinks, *why not?* Shots were starting to look good.

The game soon goes pear-shaped.

Annette and Archie are a formidable team, accustomed to winning at any cost, buy every property they land on, a strategy considered unfair by Lana and Liam. They were not immune to moving their token the wrong number of spaces to avoid penalty, then denying it shamelessly. When Mitch and Mel landed on Betty and Marty's Park Lane with a hotel and no-one noticed, they said nothing! Marty was distracted but why on earth didn't Betty speak up? Then they tried to convince everyone of a ridiculous rule that landing on Free Parking won them extra cash when everyone knew otherwise. As if!

Observing Billie and her mother, Archie thought they were pathetic. *Look at them, two smiling lumps, sitting there saying nothing, not even trying to win. Why didn't they inject themselves into the conversation?* He certainly had the best female in this family.

Then Marty and Mel added houses they hadn't paid for, and that was it for Leo who had been quietly playing a fair game. Giving the biggest speech he's made all day, he announces he will not play with cheats and rule breakers. He thinks the family is so caught up in their own stupidity they deserve each other.

Billie rushes after him, upset and angry at her family. The Mangoes erupt into gales of knee slapping laughter. The Apples watch and quietly enjoy. Liam sticks up for his fellow Lime brother-in-law, with an outburst that he too had had enough of their deceitful ways. And that's when Lana, now fuelled by a cocktail of champagne and shots, blurts out, 'Well, at least none of them have had an affair, Liam!' There is a moment when the world stops and the family tableau freezes into silence. Liam hears blood whoosh in his ears as his wife's words spin through the air and crash to the ground, shattering into a million tiny pieces.

Annette eyes widen, and Archie smiles in victory. They would have won anyway.

Christmas night

Marty and Mitch are taking a break from champagne and shots and slowing down with a few beers in the kitchen, still laughing uproariously at Liam's affair. Liam for God's sake! Brilliant. As they chat, they steal tiny spoonsful of Annette's perfect trifle which took her hours to make and set up. Annette is so uppity with her food and loved the attention she got from her creations. It was just a few sneaky nibbles. Pretty funny, really.

Except it wasn't. Annette was furious that her efforts had been tampered with, and even worse, she hadn't yet taken a photo for Instagram. Imbeciles. Unfortunately, her dressing down, designed to reduce two grown men to chastened schoolboys, only created more hilarity when she stormed out of the kitchen. Mangoes ... #sorrynotsorry

After eight hours of gently steaming, Liam's pudding was, for the first time ever, soggy. Did he accidentally put the lemon and orange juice in, instead of the zest? Did he add too much stout? Liam was beside himself; his pudding failure would plague him for months. The only saving grace was that Lana had finally crashed out on the couch and wasn't awake to witness the demise of the Pudding King. Anke was jubilant as her pudding took centre stage, no longer the understudy. In deference to Liam's dignity, Annette pretended she was full and declined a slice.

It seemed Christmas was done.

After Christmas

Betty left on Boxing Day and was never seen again. She had enough of Alan and had been saving up her allowance for a one-way ticket to Nicaragua where she spends her days barefoot and braless. Liam came out, has a new and rather fabulous partner Michael, and is living happily ever after. He practices cooking Christmas puddings every month. Ludwig and Anke will never have Christmas with the Berry's again, but Anke sends them Lebkuchenherzen every year. Annette and Archie retained the crown and their Monopoly. Billie and Leo celebrate Christmas every year with their son Brandon and his girlfriend. It's their happy space. Leo had the black pearl made into a ring and Billie loves it. Alan married his daughter-in-law Lana. They divorced after two years and Alan lost a house and half his super.

In a parallel universe, Christmas could have played out quite differently; not as interesting perhaps, but far less traumatic. In truth, I love these characters.

I love Annette, Archie, Alan, and Anke for their intellect, for their ability to spark and hold robust discussion, for their directness and honesty. If everyone took a slice of Apple on board there would be less miscommunication, less time wasting, and some very honest relationships. These four see problems clearly and can make fast, informed decisions. I love hanging out with them because I learn so much and it makes me strive to be smarter.

I adore Marty, Mitch, and Mel for their unbridled joy of life, their ability to think big, and their enduring curiosity. None of them hold grudges, they forgive and move on quickly from conflict or awkwardness. Their imaginations have no limits. With more Mango-ness in the world we would have more innovation, less stress, more play, and more action. When I'm with them, I believe I can do anything.

I am super fond of Liam, Lana, Leo, and Ludwig, the unsung heroes who do so much behind the scenes. They never show off. They just work their perfect order and analyse rigorously before launching into any half-baked decisions. If we thought more carefully before speaking, there would be less hurt in the world. With Lime routine and order, there are fewer surprises and less mistakes. They teach me to be more thoughtful, more organised and to allow space in my head just to be.

And who couldn't love Billie and Betty, those beautiful Bananas. Bursting with empathy and care for others, these two hold families together, provide a shoulder to cry on, sort out other people's spats. They believe that everyone has good in them, they keep the peace and they nurture our souls. With more Banana kindness in the world there would be less hatred, less poverty, and more care for what really matters. When I'm with people like Billie and Betty, I want to be a kinder, more caring and empathic person.

Chapter 12

The Last Word

Every anecdote in this book is true and told to me by real humans. The stories, however, are not from one person but a culmination of sketches from different people, compiled to create more extreme and memorable examples.

In our stories, for the most part, our Fruit lovers lived happily ever after. We know in the real world this is not always the case. I've attempted to isolate key problems that typically occur in relationships, and along the way, provide ideas and tips for working through Fruit-inspired challenges.

The thing is, if our personal, intimate relationships are reasonably healthy, we don't set out to harm and to hurt. We simply see life through our own lens, something no-one else can look through. We believe our way is the right way. If you and your partner are on opposite sides of the room with a big red ball suspended between you, one of you will swear blind it's a red ball, until you walk around to the other side and see that their half is painted blue.

It's the same with our natural traits. An Apple may consider their behaviour to be assertive; you think it's aggressive. A Mango may think they're hilarious; you think they're obnoxious. A Lime thinks they're being efficient;

you see them as cold. When a Banana thinks they are being accommodating; you see them as weak.

Long term relationships can be arduous, and the passing of time and different life stages and circumstances present new challenges and we don't always show up with our best self.

We live in a world where our work demands so much of us in terms of time, technology, and relationships. By the time we arrive home, we can't be bothered with simple courtesy and the niceties that are part of a healthy relationship. And yet home is where our most important relationships reside.

When things get tricky between us, we default to our worst selves. I should know. I teach this for a living, and I can assure you in the heat of an argument I am reminded time and again this is true. Sometimes though, I just want to be petulant and badly behaved. This is reality, my friends. The ups and downs. Without the downs, we can't go up.

Empathy is our secret superpower.

You will never love everything about anyone.

You will never find the perfect partner. You are not the perfect partner.

The perfect partner does not exist. So stop looking.

But when you find someone special, someone you don't want to let go, you must love them for who they are, not for who you want them to become. And before we can even begin to love someone else, you know what they say, you have to love yourself. Dr Seuss says it best:

"Today you are You, that is truer than true. There is no one alive who is Youer than You."

—Dr Seuss

You are a unique, beautiful human, a combination of Apple, Mango, Lime, and Banana. Whatever your strengths, whatever your blend, you have a responsibility to yourself to be the best self you can be. When we understand and respect each other's differences, we can connect with our hearts and our minds, and together we become a formidable, unstoppable team.

It's a wonderful feeling. Here's to Fruitful relationships.

More Information

Here is a bunch of experts and resources in the field of relationships, sexuality, love, gender differences, and divorce. Check out their books, blogs, articles, TED talks, and podcasts.

Australia and New Zealand

Ferrari M (2020) 'Melissa Ferrari, 'accessed 2 September 2020

McKimmie I (2017) 'Isiah McKimmie, Couples Therapist, Sex Therapist, Sexologist + Coach,' accessed 2 September 2020

Luna Blue Author (2020) @lunablueauthor (twitter), accessed 2 September 2020

Britain and Europe

Go Dates (2020) 'Go Dates', accessed 2 September 2020

Perel E (2020) 'Esther Perel,' accessed 2 September 2020

Canada and USA

Bobby LM (2020) 'Growing Self-Counselling and Coaching,' Growing Self, US, accessed 2 September 2020

Chapman G (2020) 'The 5 Love Languages,' Northfield Publishing, US, accessed 2 September 2020

Creager T (2020) 'Making the World Safe for Love,' accessed 2 September 2020

Crossley T (2020) 'Blog Articles & Podcasts In Tracy's Words,' accessed 2 September 2020

Fisher H (2020) 'Helen Fisher PhD,' accessed 2 September 2020.

Masini A (2020) 'April Masini,' Masini Enterprises, US, accessed 2 September 2020

Overstreet E (2018) 'Elizabeth Overstreet; Relationship Expert,' accessed 2 September 2020

With Thanks

To my dear friend and superstar editor, Jane O'Connell, I cannot express my gratitude enough. It was such a pleasure to work with someone who knows me so well and allowed me to keep my voice. She helped turn a bunch of words into something with meaning, and has almost made me delete the word "stuff" from my vocabulary. Almost.

To the team at Ocean Reeve Publishing who've helped with so many aspects of the publishing process, you are the knight in shining armour to the self publishing author.

A special thanks to the patient Banana/Lime Sarah-Kate Hill who guided me through and tolerated my Apple sharpness.

To Jozzelle de Jesus from E-Studios, for my beloved Fruit characters, thank you. They are now permanent voices in my head.

And to all the men I've loved before. Well, maybe just the current one, in an effort to be less Mango. My darling Terry, thank you for not only providing some brilliant material for this book but showing me that although there is no such thing as a perfect relationship, working hard at it makes it all worthwhile.

About Lynne

If you've ever been asked if you are an Apple, Mango, Lime, or Banana, it's likely you've encountered the work of renowned business speaker and facilitator Lynne Schinella, who created the Fruit Personality Profiling System in 2004, which is used by hundreds of companies across Australia.

Lynne works with teams to help them function more effectively, for less stress, greater productivity, and more fun!

Author of *Bite Me! and other Do's and Don'ts of Dealing with our Differences*, Lynne pens a regular blog series and hosts two podcasts **Fruitful Conversations** and **Fruitful Pairs**.

Pick Me! Loving and Living with People You Just Don't Get is Lynne's second book.

In between facilitating workshops with organisations, Lynne loves to bake up a storm, often sharing her creations online. Lynne has two grown up sons and is based in beautiful Brunswick Heads in NSW Australia where she lives with her partner.

For enquiries about Lynne's workplace programs, or to have her speak at your business event, please contact support@lynneschinella.com.au.

More information at www.lynneschinella.com.au.

Connect with Lynne on LinkedIn, Facebook, and Instagram.